S0-BDS-347

Table of Contents

Name _____

Date _____ Class _____

Using the Map Key

A map key explains what the symbols, shading, and colors on a map represent. Symbols range from simple dots and circles that represent cities and capitals to tiny drawings that represent types of industry or agriculture. Shading and colors are used to show elevation, population density, political divisions, and so on. The map key for the map of China below uses a combination of shading and drawings to represent economic activity and resources.

Directions: Study the map and the map key. Then, answer the questions that follow.

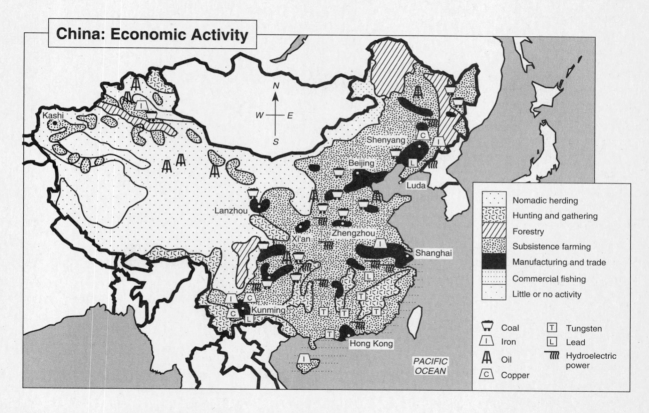

1. What does the solid black shading represent? _____

2. What kind of shading is used to represent commercial fishing? _____

3. Where does commercial fishing take place, according to the map? _____

4. What symbol is used to represent oil? _____

5. In what part of China is oil found? _____

6. What kind of activity is represented by slanted parallel lines? _____

7. In what part of China are the largest forests found? _____

8. What resource is found in the part of China that surrounds Hong Kong? _____

Map and Globe Skills

Using the Compass Rose

Most maps include a symbol to tell you which direction on the map is north.
On some maps, the symbol is a single arrow pointing toward the letter *N*.
The *N* stands for North, and the arrow is pointing toward the North Pole.
You can figure out the other directions from that single arrow.

Other maps show the four main directions of the compass—north, east,
south, and west. These are called the cardinal directions. However, some
maps provide a compass rose that indicates intermediate directions as well
as the cardinal directions. Intermediate directions are northeast, southeast,
southwest, and northwest.

Directions: Study the compass rose and the map of Australia beside it.
Then, answer the questions that follow.

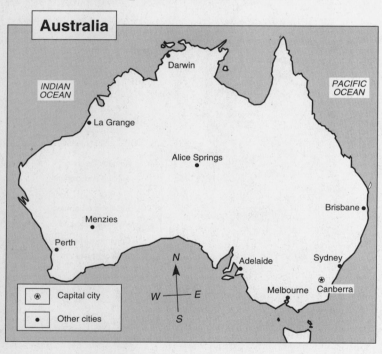

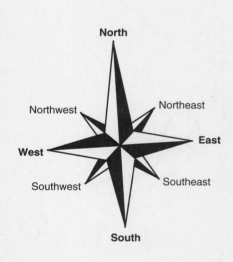

1. What is the direction from Alice Springs to Darwin? _____

2. What direction would you be taking if you traveled from Sydney to Alice Springs?

_____

3. In what direction would you go to get from Perth to Menzies? _____

4. Darwin is on the northern coast of Australia. On what coast is Melbourne located?

_____

5. On what coast is Brisbane located? _____

6. If you flew across Australia from La Grange to Sydney, in what direction would you be

traveling? _____

Using the Map Scale

A map is always much smaller than the area it represents. In order to figure out distances when using a map, you need to know the scale of the map. The scale on a map tells you the relationship between a distance on a map and the real distance on the earth's surface. You measure a distance on the map. Then, you use the scale to convert it to the real distance.

Directions: Study the map and the map scale below. Then, use a ruler along with either a piece of string or the edge of a piece of paper to measure distances and to answer the questions.

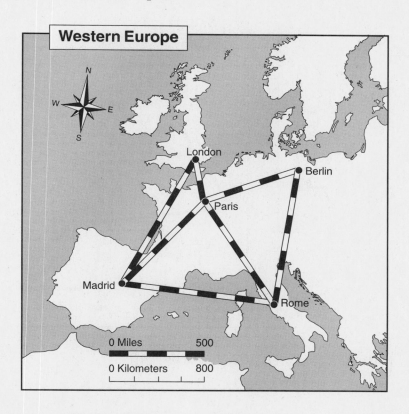

1. How many miles is it from London to Madrid? _____

   How many kilometers? _____

2. If you were to fly directly from Rome to Paris and then on to Berlin, how many miles would you travel? _____

3. Which city is farther from Paris, Madrid or Berlin? _____

4. If you were to travel from London to Rome via Paris and back again by the same route, how many miles would you travel? _____

5. How many kilometers would you go if you flew from Madrid to Rome? _____

Map and Globe Skills

Comparing Maps of Different Scale

The scale of a map shows you how a distance on the map relates to the actual distance on the earth's surface. A small-scale map shows a large area; a large-scale map shows a smaller area in greater detail. Map A below is a small-scale map of part of Southwest Asia; Map B is a larger-scale map of Kuwait.

Directions: Study the two maps below, and answer the questions that follow.

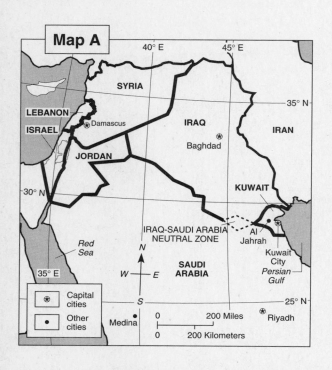

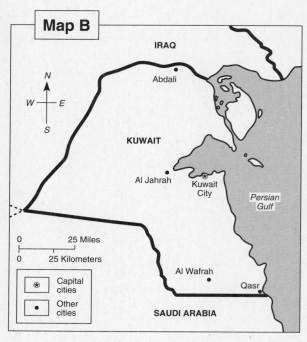

1. What does Map A tell you about Kuwait that Map B does not?

   _____

   _____

2. What does Map B tell you about Kuwait that Map A does not?

   _____

   _____

3. Which map would you use to describe Kuwait's position in relation to other countries of Southwest Asia?

   _____

4. Which map would you use to determine the distance from Kuwait City to Al Wafrah?

   _____

Understanding Hemispheres

The word *hemisphere* means half of a sphere. The earth can be divided into hemispheres in two different ways. When it is divided along the Equator, the two hemispheres are the Northern Hemisphere and the Southern Hemisphere. When it is divided along the Prime Meridian from the North Pole to the South Pole, the two hemispheres are the Western Hemisphere and the Eastern Hemisphere.

Directions: Study the illustrations of the earth's hemispheres below. Then, answer the questions that follow.

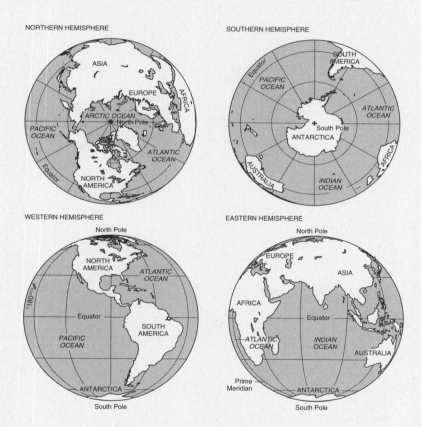

1. In which two hemispheres is the United States located? _____

2. What is the line that divides the Northern Hemisphere from the Southern Hemisphere?

   _____

3. In which two hemispheres is Australia located? _____

4. Which ocean is not found in the Western Hemisphere? _____

5. Which hemisphere is the only one in which Antarctica is not found? _____

Map and Globe Skills

Understanding Grids

Maps often have grids drawn on them to help you find the exact location of a place. A grid is a system of horizontal and vertical lines that cross each other to form squares. The squares are labeled with numbers from left to right and with letters from top to bottom. That way, each square has its own number/letter combination. A grid map of a city zoo appears below.

Directions: Study the map and the grid below. Then, answer the questions that follow.

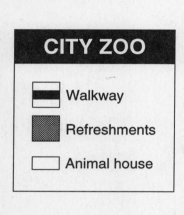

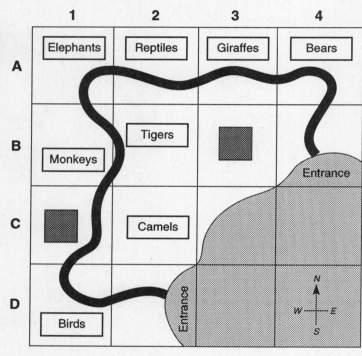

1. In what square are the bears located? _____

2. What animals are located in A3? _____

3. In what two squares are the zoo entrances? _____

4. If you were to follow the walkway from the west entrance to the elephant house, what squares would you pass through? _____

5. What squares would you pass through if you came in at the north entrance and followed the walkway to the elephant house? _____

Map and Globe Skills

Using a Map Grid

Map grids are very useful for locating places on a street map or a road map. Imagine that you arrive in a city you've never visited before and that you need to locate a particular street. You don't want to read all of the street names on the map to find the one you need. Instead, you use the map index. The map index will give the number and the letter of the square in which the street you want is located. Once you find the correct square, you will find the street in that square.

Directions: Study the street map of Lima, Peru, and the index to some of its main buildings. Then, answer the questions that follow.

Lima, Peru

Rimac River

Index

1 Church of Santa Rosa, A1
2 Church of Santo Domingo, A2
3 Government Palace, A3
4 San Francisco Church, A3
5 City Hall, A2
6 Archbishop's Palace, A3
7 Cathedral, B3
8 Congress, A4
9 Church of Las Nazarenas, C1
10 Municipal Theater, B1
11 Church of San Augustin, B2
12 Church of La Merced, C3
13 Trinity Church, C3
14 Church of Jesus Maria, C2
15 San Marcos University, D4

1. At the intersection of which two streets is the Church of Santa Rosa? _____

2. What is the grid location of San Marcos University? _____

3. If you were walking from the Church of La Merced to Trinity Church, what avenue would you walk along? _____

4. What street would you take to get from the Church of San Augustin to the Church of Jesus Maria? _____

5. If you were telling someone the location of the building where Congress meets, what two streets would you name? _____

Map and Globe Skills

Understanding Latitude and Longitude

Lines of latitude and longitude work somewhat like a map grid, but on a global scale. These two sets of imaginary lines circle the globe. Lines of latitude run east and west; lines of longitude run north and south. Together, they form a grid. Locations on these lines are stated in degrees. Each degree is divided into 60 minutes.

　　Lines of latitude are also called parallels because they are parallel to each other. The Equator is located at 0° latitude. All the other lines of latitude are said to be so many degrees north or south of the Equator.

　　Lines of longitude are also called meridians. All lines of longitude pass through the North Pole and the South Pole. The line for 0° longitude passes through Greenwich, England. It is called the Prime Meridian. All other lines of longitude are measured in degrees east or west of the Prime Meridian. East and west meridians meet at 180° in the Pacific Ocean.

Directions: Study the illustrations of latitude and longitude below. Then, answer the questions that follow.

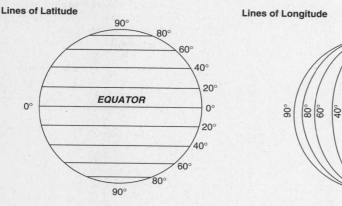

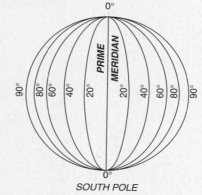

1. What are two names for the lines that run north to south?

    _____

    _____

2. What are two names for the lines that run east to west?

    _____

    _____

3. What would be the line of latitude for a place that is halfway between the Equator and the North Pole?

    _____

4. What would be the line of longitude for a place that is west of the Prime Meridian, halfway between the Prime Meridian and the 180° line of longitude?

    _____

Using Latitude and Longitude

Every place on earth has two points, or coordinates, that mark its location. These coordinates are measured in degrees of latitude and degrees of longitude. Imagine that you want to find out where Beijing, China, is. You start with the index section of an atlas. This index gives you not only the page number of the map of China, but also the coordinates for Beijing: 40°N, 116°E. So you know that when you turn to the map of China, you will look for the line of latitude marked 40°N. Then, you will look in the area between 110°E and 120°E and you will find Beijing.

Directions: The map of Australia below shows lines of latitude and lines of longitude, each labeled in degrees. Give the approximate locations of the cities listed below the map.

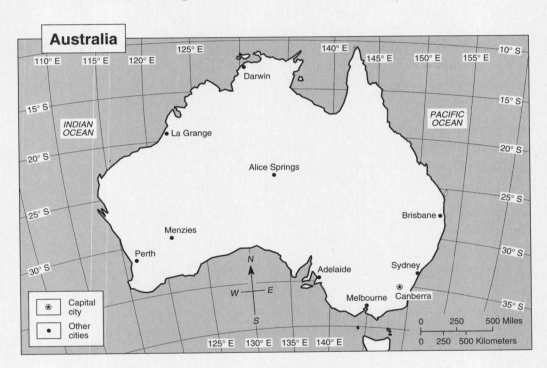

	Latitude	Longitude
1. Canberra	_____	_____
2. Melbourne	_____	_____
3. Darwin	_____	_____
4. Perth	_____	_____
5. Brisbane	_____	_____

Map and Globe Skills

Comparing Globes and Maps

Globes and maps are used frequently in geography. To make the best possible use of maps and globes, you need to understand how they relate to one another and what kind of information each can provide.

Directions: Read the information about globes and maps below. Then, answer the questions that follow. Use a separate piece of paper for your answers.

Globes. A globe is the most accurate way of showing the world's surface. It is a scale model of the earth, showing actual shapes, relative sizes, and locations of landmasses and bodies of water. A globe also provides accurate information about distances and directions between two points. Globes, however, are very small representations of the earth. Even a large globe cannot show much detail. Also, globes are difficult to carry around, and you can look at only one half of a globe at any one time.

Maps. Maps are flat representations of the curved surface of the earth. Because they are flat, they can be shown in a book. They can be folded up and used for planning trips. They can show very large areas or very small areas. They are flexible tools that can provide large amounts of information very efficiently. Maps are not as accurate as globes, however. To create a flat representation of the curved surface of the earth, something has to be distorted. You can understand this by studying the illustration below. The surface of the globe has been "peeled off" and cut along the lines of longitude. The resulting map is not easy to read.

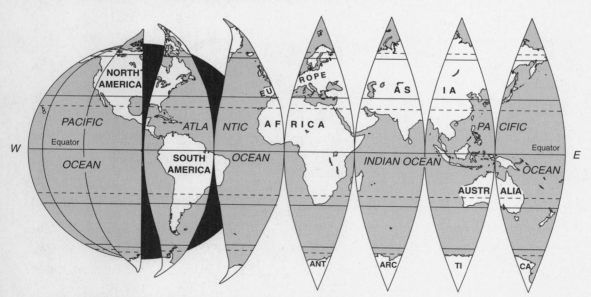

1. What advantage does a globe have over a flat map?
2. What are the main disadvantages of a globe?
3. What advantages do maps have over globes?
4. Why are maps less accurate than globes?
5. What does the illustration on this page tell you?

© Prentice-Hall, Inc.

Understanding Projection

The method used to show the curved surface of the earth as a flat map is called a projection. The three most common kinds of projections are based on different ways of placing a piece of paper around the globe and "pulling" the images off the globe and onto the paper. Other projections are based on mathematical formulas.

Directions: Study the projections described and illustrated below. Then, answer the questions that follow. Use a separate piece of paper for your answers.

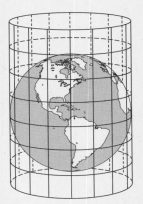

Cylindrical Projection

Conic Projection

Flat-Plane Projection

Cylindrical Projection. This projection is made by placing a rectangular piece of paper around the globe so that it touches the Equator. Lines of longitude that meet at the poles on a globe are parallel. The areas near the poles are distorted and look much larger than they really are.

Conic Projection. Here, a cone-shaped piece of paper is placed over the globe. The areas where the paper touches the globe are most accurately represented. Those near the tip of the globe are most distorted.

Flat-Plane Projection. Here a flat piece of paper is placed against the globe. The map is accurate at the point of contact. Distortion increases as you move away from the center. Flat-plane projections are often used to show polar regions.

Other Projections. An example of a map based on a mathematical formula is the Robinson projection, which balances different kinds of distortion to make maps that are easy to read.

1. What is a map projection?

2. Which areas of the earth are most distorted on a cylindrical projection?

3. Which kind of projection is often used to show polar areas?

4. Which projection, based on mathematical formulas, balances different kinds of distortions?

Map and Globe Skills

Great Circles and Straight Lines

Travelers flying from London to New York are often surprised to hear the captain announce that they are flying over Nova Scotia in Canada. "Why aren't we going straight across the Atlantic?" they ask, thinking of the route they have seen on a flat map. The reason is the captain has taken the great-circle route: the shortest distance between the two cities.

Directions: Read the information about great circles, and study the illustrations below. Then, complete the activities, and answer the questions.

The shortest distance between any two points on a globe can be found by stretching a string between them. To find the shortest distance using maps, you need to understand projection and distortion. Look at the two maps below. The cylindrical projection on the left suggests that the shortest distance between Philadelphia and Beijing is a straight east-west line. Compare this with the flat-plane polar projection on the right. Here, you see that the great-circle route across the North Pole is the shortest route.

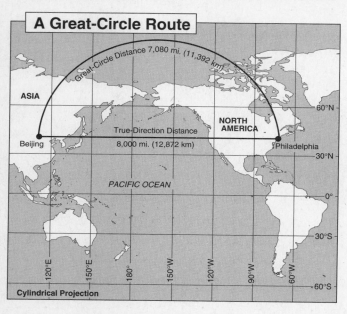

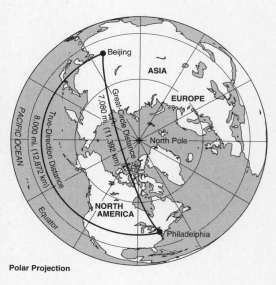

1. Which of the two maps would be more helpful to an airline pilot flying from Philadelphia to Beijing? Why? _____

2. Imagine that you are going to fly west from Moscow to San Francisco. Look at a physical map of the world. Which countries does the map suggest you will fly over?

   _____

3. Now, use a globe and a piece of string to plot the straight-line, or great-circle, route between Moscow and San Francisco. Which countries would you actually fly over?

   _____

4. What does this activity reveal about maps? _____

Maps With Accurate Shapes: Conformal Maps

Directions: Read the information about conformal maps, and study the map below. Then, answer the questions that follow.

Conformal maps are so named because the shapes of the landmasses conform to, or look like, the shapes that appear on the globe. Directions are also correct. However, distances and size are greatly distorted, especially in the polar regions. Lines of latitude and longitude cross at right angles. The lines of longitude that meet at the poles on a globe, however, are parallel on this map. The Mercator projection below is an example of a conformal map.

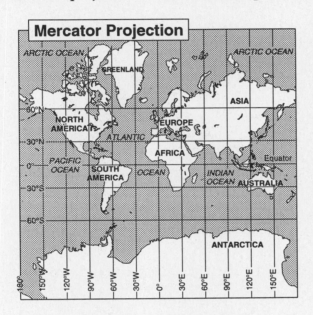

1. Use a globe to compare the size of Antarctica on this map with the size of that continent on the globe. What do you observe?

   _____

   _____

2. Look at the comparative sizes of Greenland and Africa on the map and on the globe. What do you observe?

   _____

   _____

3. Which aspects of this map are correct and which are distorted?

   _____

   _____

4. Why do you think this projection is often used for making navigational charts?

   _____

Maps With Accurate Areas: Equal-Area Maps

Directions: Read the information about equal-area maps, and study the map below. Then, answer the questions that follow.

Equal-area maps show the correct sizes of landmasses in relation to other landmasses. A nation that is twice the size of another nation will appear that way on the map. However, in order to depict correct size, an equal-area map distorts both shape and direction. The Mollweide projection below is an example of an equal-area map.

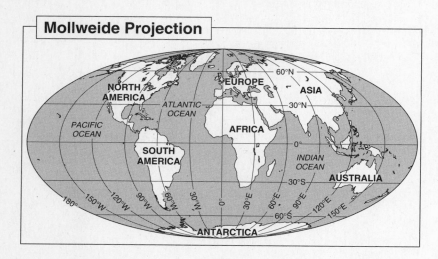

1. Which aspects of this map are correct and which are distorted?

_____

_____

_____

2. Describe the lines of longitude on this map.

_____

_____

_____

3. Compare the shape of North America on this map with the shape of North America on a globe. What do you observe?

_____

_____

_____

Name	
Date	Class

Maps With Accurate Distances: Equidistant Maps

Directions: Read the information about equidistant maps, and study the maps below. Then, answer the questions that follow.

Equidistant maps show the correct distance between places. Maps of the world can never show all distances accurately because it is not possible to show the correct lengths of all lines of latitude and longitude. Small areas, however, can be mapped with little distortion of distance. The maps below are examples of equidistant maps. On both maps, the scale is large enough that the maps could be used to measure distances accurately.

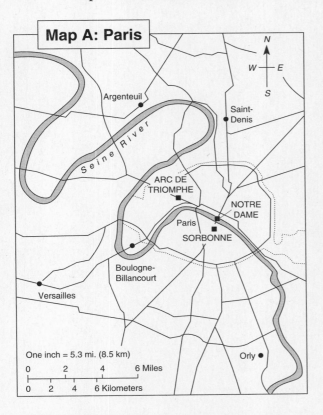

Map A: Paris

One inch = 5.3 mi. (8.5 km)

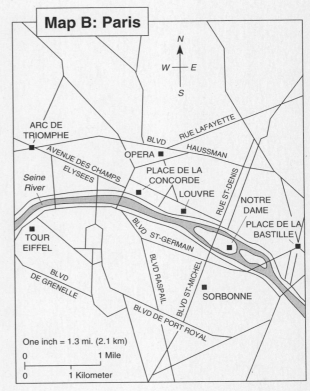

Map B: Paris

One inch = 1.3 mi. (2.1 km)

1. What does an equidistant map show correctly? _____

2. Why would it not be possible to have an equidistant map of the world? _____
_____

3. What kind of areas lend themselves to equidistant maps? _____
_____

4. What kinds of distances could you measure on Map A above? _____
_____

5. What kinds of distances could you measure on Map B? _____
_____

Map and Globe Skills

Maps With Accurate Directions: Azimuthal Maps

Directions: Read the information about azimuthal maps, and study the map. Then, answer the questions that follow.

   Azimuthal maps show direction correctly. Shape and size are distorted, with the greatest distortions on the outer edges of the map. Azimuthal maps are circular and often have the North Pole or the South Pole as their central point. The azimuthal projection below has the North Pole as its central point.

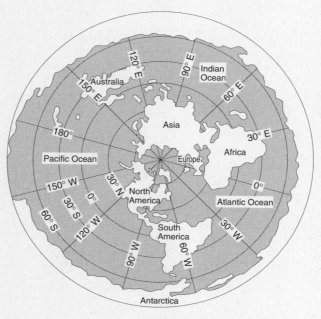

Azimuthal Projection

1. What does an azimuthal map show correctly? _____

2. What is distorted on this type of map? _____
   _____

3. Which continent on the map above is most distorted? _____

4. What direction would you take from the North Pole if you wanted to fly through the center of South America?
   _____

5. What direction would you take from the North Pole to reach Central America?
   _____

Reading a Political Map

A political map shows political features such as national or state boundaries, capital cities and other major cities. Some political maps use color to differentiate countries or states. The map of Western Europe below is an example of a political map.

Directions: Study the map and the key below. Then, answer the questions that follow.

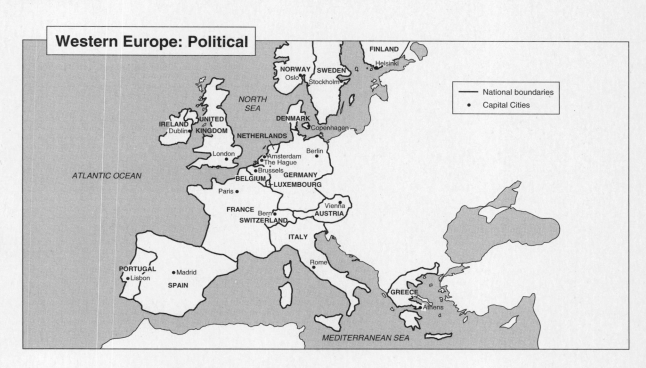

Western Europe: Political

1. What does a solid black line on the map signify? _____
2. Which nations of Western Europe border on the Mediterranean Sea?

   _____

   _____

3. List the nations that share a border with Switzerland.

   _____

   _____

4. What is the capital of Spain? _____
5. What is the capital of Germany? _____
6. Which country lies closest to the North African coast? _____

Map and Globe Skills

Elevation on a Map

Elevation refers to the height of land above sea level. Mountains are the landforms with the highest elevation. Elevation is shown on maps by different colors or different types of shading. On a color map, lower elevations are generally shown in different shades of green, while higher elevations are shown in shades of brown. On the map of Canada below, different elevations are indicated by different types of patterns. The lighter the pattern, the higher the elevation.

Directions: Study the map and the map key below. Then, answer the questions.

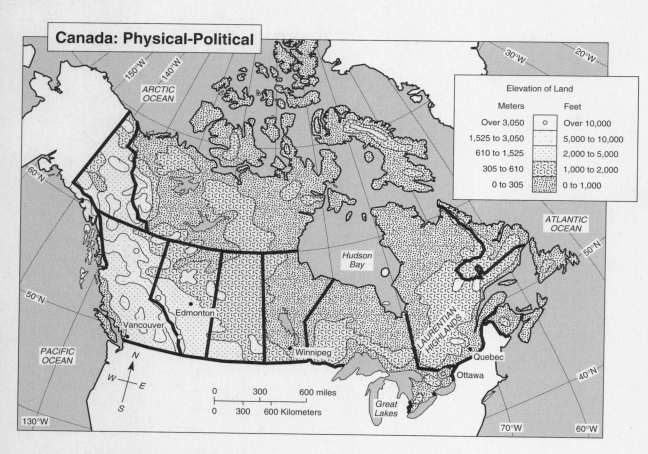

1. In which area of Canada are the highest elevations found? _____

2. What is the elevation of most of the land around Hudson Bay? _____

3. Which city is at a higher elevation, Quebec or Edmonton? _____

4. What kinds of landforms would you expect to find in the western part of Canada?

_____

Four Types of Landforms

Landforms are features that are found on the earth's surface. There are four main types of landforms: mountains, hills, plateaus, and plains. The diagram and the key below show the four types.

Directions: Study the diagram and the key below, and read the descriptions of landforms. Then, answer the questions.

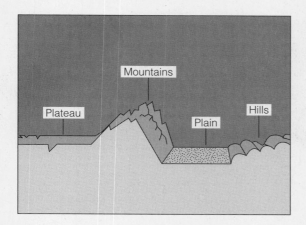

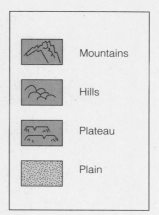

Mountains. Mountains have the highest elevations of all landforms. They usually have steep slopes and a small summit. Mountains that form a line are called a range. The highest mountains in the world are the Himalayas. The hills around mountains are called foothills because they lie at the foot of the mountains.

Hills. Hills, like mountains, rise above the land around them, but they are generally lower and less steep than mountains. Rivers and lakes are often found in hilly areas. There is very little level land in hilly areas.

Plateaus. Plateaus are areas of level land at a high elevation. Plateaus are often called tablelands because they resemble giant tabletops. If a river has worn a deep gap into a plateau, the opening is called a canyon.

Plains. Plains consist of flat, or almost flat, land, usually at low elevations. Coastal plains are found along coasts, and floodplains are found along most large rivers.

1. What is the difference between mountains and hills?

   _____

2. In what ways are plateaus and plains similar, and in what ways are they different?

   _____

3. What is a canyon? _____

4. What symbol is used here to indicate a plain? _____

5. Why would farmers be more likely to farm on a plain than on hilly ground?

   _____

Map and Globe Skills

Relief on a Map

A relief map shows the location of major landforms. Some relief maps use shading and symbols to indicate different types of landforms. Others use a technique called shaded relief to show mountain ranges. With shaded relief, the location of mountains can be seen at a glance because the area they cover is shaded as if with a pencil. The relief map of Eastern Europe below uses shaded relief.

Directions: Study the map and the map key below. Then, answer the questions.

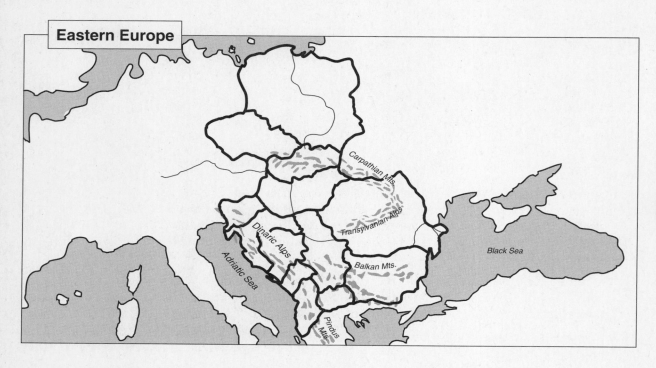

Eastern Europe

1. Locate the mountainous regions in Eastern Europe. Describe their location.

   _____

   _____

2. Which mountain ranges run through the center of the region?

   _____

3. What information does shaded relief provide, and what information is not provided?

   _____

Maps of the Ocean Floor

Maps of the ocean floor show that there are mountains and valleys under the oceans as well as on land. Many small islands are actually the tops of underwater mountains. The map below shows the ocean floor of the Atlantic.

Directions: Study the map below. Then, use an atlas to help you answer the questions. Use a separate piece of paper for the answers to the first two questions.

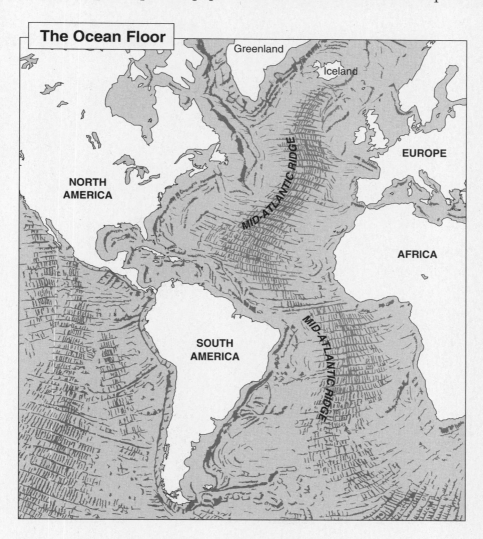

The Ocean Floor

1. What is the name of the mountain range that runs through the Atlantic from north to south?

2. Name three island groups off the northwest coast of Africa that are the tops of mountains.

3. Circle and label the island of Cuba on the map above.

4. Circle and label the Falkland Islands.

5. Circle and label the Galápagos Islands.

Map and Globe Skills

Reading a Time Zone Map

A time zone map helps you figure out what time it is in different parts of the world. There are 24 time zones altogether—one for each hour of the day. Four of the 24 time zones are shown in the map of North Africa below. The band across the top is a key to the actual time in each time zone. The band across the bottom tells you how many hours to add or subtract for each time zone. It shows that you add an hour for each time zone as you move from west to east.

Directions: Study the map below. Then, answer the questions that follow.

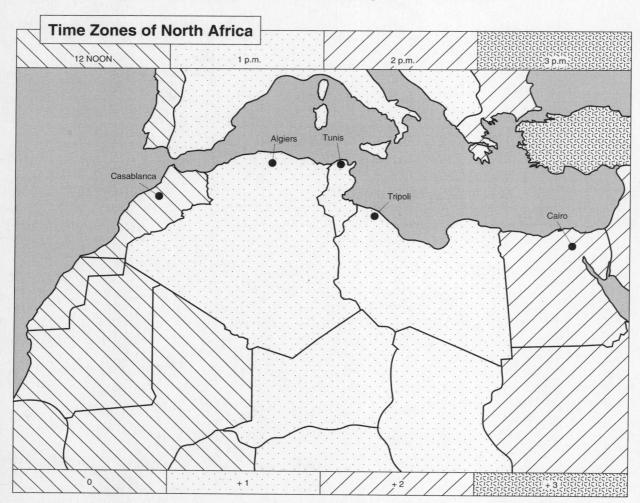

Time Zones of North Africa

12 NOON   1 p.m.   2 p.m.   3 p.m.

Casablanca   Algiers   Tunis   Tripoli   Cairo

0   + 1   + 2   + 3

1. If it is 6 P.M. in Cairo, what time is it in a city two time zones to the west? _____

2. If it is 2 A.M. in Tunis, what time is it in Casablanca? _____

3. When it is 12 noon in Algiers, what time is it in Tripoli? _____

4. When it is midnight in Tunis, what time is it in Cairo? _____

5. When it is 5 P.M. in Tripoli, what time is it in the zone labeled + 3? _____

        Social Studies Skills Handbook

Name _____

Date _____ Class _____

Reading a Natural Vegetation Map

A natural vegetation map tells you what plants grow naturally in places that have not been altered significantly by human activity. The map below shows the natural vegetation regions of the mainland United States.

Directions: Study the map and the map key below. Then, answer the questions that follow. You may wish to consult an atlas.

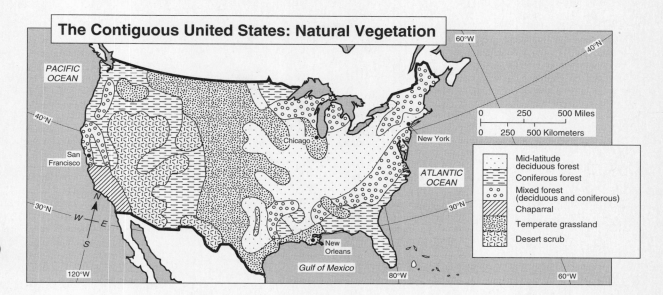

1. What is the natural vegetation of the area where you live?

   _____

2. What is the natural vegetation of the Great Plains?

   _____

3. If you were going to northern New England, what vegetation would you expect to find?

   _____

4. In the southern part of which state is chaparral the natural vegetation?

   _____

5. What kind of forest would you find in the Rocky Mountains?

   _____

6. What do the state of Washington and the state of Florida have in common?

   _____

Name _____

Date _____ Class _____

Map and Globe Skills

Reading a Climate Map

Climate maps divide the world into climate regions. Each type of climate region has specific patterns of temperature, precipitation, and wind. The map below shows the climate regions of the British Isles and the Nordic nations.

Directions: Study the map and the map key below. Then, answer the questions that follow.

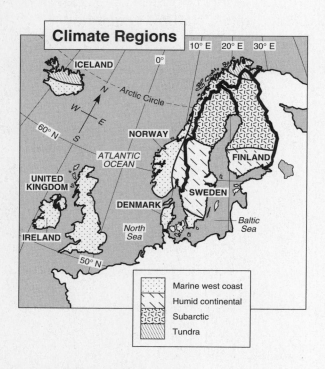

1. What is the climate region of the British Isles?

   _____

2. What three climate regions are found in Finland?

   _____

3. Which climate region is found in the northernmost parts of the area shown on the map?

   _____

4. If you were to travel from the west coast of Norway to the east coast of Sweden, at about 60°N latitude, which climate regions would you experience?

   _____

5. Which of the countries shown have a subarctic climate region?

   _____

Reading an Economic Activity Map

An economic activity map shows general information about how people make a living in different parts of a region. The map below shows economic activity in West and Central Africa.

Directions: Study the map and the map key below. Then, answer the questions that follow. You may wish to use an atlas to help you locate places.

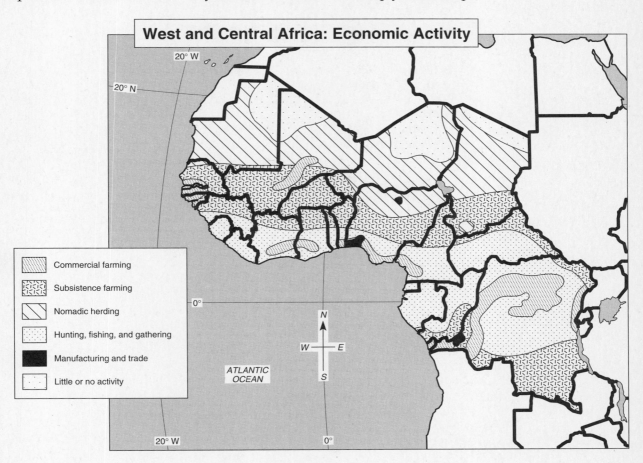

1. What is the main economic activity in the northern part of the area shown? _____

2. What four economic activities are practiced in Zaire? _____

   _____

3. What activity occupies the most land in the southern half of the region? _____

4. Which country has the most manufacturing and trade? _____

5. What three activities are practiced in Mali? _____

6. What reasons can you offer for the lack of variety of economic activity in the northern part of the region? _____

   _____

Map and Globe Skills

Reading a Historical Map

A historical map tells you what was happening in a region at an earlier time in history. Comparing a historical map with a map of the present day can help you to understand the impact of history. The map below shows Africa south of the Sahara in 1914, when most parts of the continent were European colonies.

Directions: Study the map and the map key below. Then, answer the questions that follow. You may wish to refer to a map of present-day Africa in an atlas to help you locate places.

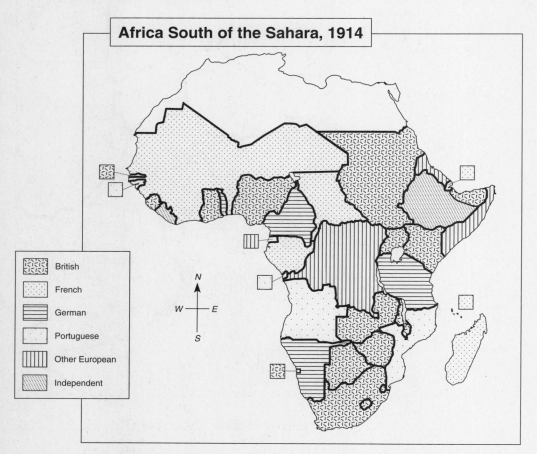

Africa South of the Sahara, 1914

British
French
German
Portuguese
Other European
Independent

1. Which European country controlled much of the southern part of the region in 1914? _____

2. Which present-day countries were controlled by the Portuguese? _____

3. Which two countries remained independent in 1914? _____

4. Which European country controlled Madagascar and the Comoro Islands? _____

5. What do present-day Namibia, Cameroon, and Tanzania have in common? _____

Social Studies Skills Handbook

Understanding Isolines

Maps can show you the ways the parts of a place are similar and different with isolines. Isolines are lines on a map that connect points of equal value. Isolines can show elevation, for example, by connecting points on the map that have the same elevation. Another common use of isolines is on a temperature map, where the isolines connect areas of equal temperature.

Directions: Read the information about isolines, and study the map below. Then, answer the questions. Use a separate piece of paper for your answers.

A contour map is one type of map that uses isolines. *Contour* means outline or shape. An isoline connects all points where the elevation is the same. If you were to hike along an isoline, you would always be at the same height above sea level. Each isoline is labeled with a number that tells the number of feet or meters above sea level along that isoline.

The arrangement of the isolines tells you how steep the land is. When a series of isolines is close together, it means that the terrain is steep. Isolines that are far apart indicate that the land is relatively flat.

There are no isolines at sea level, where the elevation is 0 feet above sea level. Rivers always run downhill, so they always cross isolines. Lakes are flat, so they never cross isolines. The map below shows the isolines on a small island.

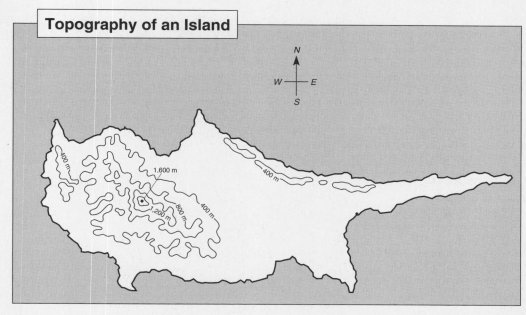

Topography of an Island

1. What are isolines?
2. What arrangement of isolines on a contour map would tell you that the land is steep? Explain why this is so.
3. What is the highest elevation on the island?
4. In which area of the island is the land steepest?
5. Which area of the island has the flattest land?

Name _____

Date _____ Class _____

Map and Globe Skills

Reading a Contour Map

Directions: A contour map tells you about elevation and relief. The contour map below shows Lord Howe Island in the South Pacific. Study the map and the map key below. Then, answer the questions.

1. What elevation, in meters, does the first isoline inland from the coast represent?

   _____

2. What is the elevation of the highest point on Lord Howe Island?

   _____

3. Are "Big Slope" and "The Saddle" at the same elevation or at different ones?

   _____

4. Is the island generally steeper near its northern part or near its southern part?

   _____

5. Where is the steepest part of the island?

   _____

6. Does the northern or southern side of Mount Gower have the more gradual increase in elevation?

   _____

7. Imagine that you want to climb to the top of Mount Gower. Describe how you would approach the mountain for a relatively gradual ascent.

   _____

   _____

   _____

   _____

   _____

   _____

   _____

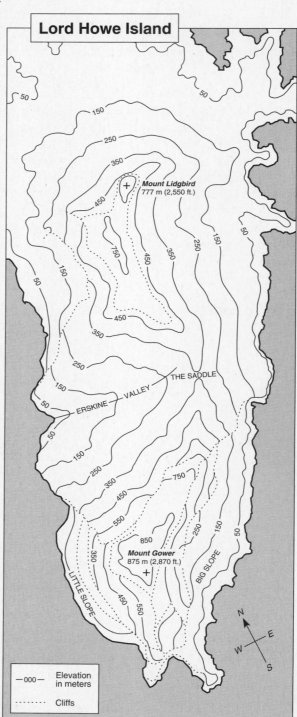

Lord Howe Island

Mount Lidgbird
777 m (2,550 ft.)

THE SADDLE

ERSKINE VALLEY

BIG SLOPE

LITTLE SLOPE

Mount Gower
875 m (2,870 ft.)

— 000   Elevation in meters

······   Cliffs

© Prentice-Hall, Inc.

Social Studies Skills Handbook

Name _____

Date _____ Class _____

Reading a Population Density Map

Another type of map that uses isolines is a population density map. The isolines on a population density map outline the areas with similar population densities. A population density map shows which parts of a region are heavily populated and which parts are sparsely or lightly populated. The map key tells you how many people live in each square mile or square kilometer of the region shown. The map below shows the population density of Australia.

Directions: Study the map and the map key below. Then, answer the questions that follow. You may need to use a physical map of Australia in an atlas to answer some of the questions.

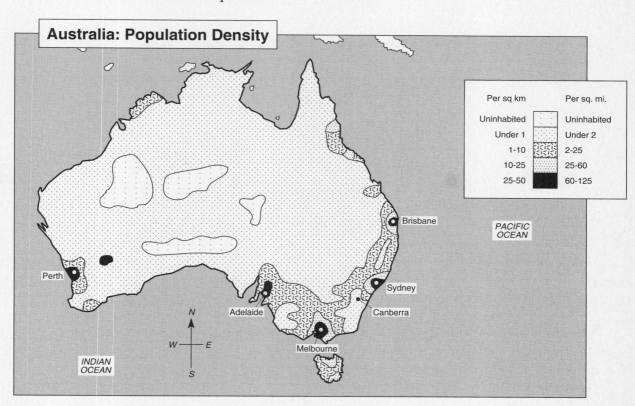

1. According to the key, what is the population density of most of Australia? _____

2. What regions of Australia are the most densely populated? _____

_____

3. Why do you think the most densely populated areas are mainly on the coast of Australia? _____

4. Study Australia's river system on a physical map. Then suggest reasons for the concentration of population in the southeastern corner of Australia. _____

_____

Map and Globe Skills

Reading a Temperature Map

Temperature maps also use isolines to show temperature patterns around the world. Some temperature maps show normal temperatures in a particular month, such as July or January. Others, like the map below, show average temperatures over the year. On this map, the varied shadings indicate hot, temperate, and cold areas. Actual temperatures, in degrees Fahrenheit, appear on the right and left edges of the map.

Directions: Study the map and the map key below. Then, answer the questions.

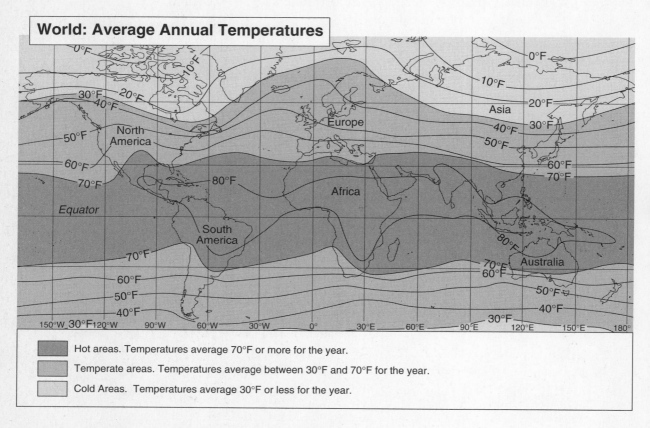

World: Average Annual Temperatures

Hot areas. Temperatures average 70°F or more for the year.

Temperate areas. Temperatures average between 30°F and 70°F for the year.

Cold Areas. Temperatures average 30°F or less for the year.

1. Which part of the world has the hottest average temperatures? _____

2. Which part has the coolest average temperatures? _____

3. What is the average annual temperature range for most of the continent of Africa?

   _____

4. What is the average annual temperature range for most of Europe? _____

Map and Globe Skills

Reading a Population Distribution Map

A population distribution map shows how the population is spread out over an area of land. Each dot on a map represents a specific number of people. The areas that have many dots are densely populated; those that have few dots are sparsely populated. The map below shows the population distribution of Mexico.

Directions: Study the map and the map key below. Use a political map of Mexico to help you answer the questions.

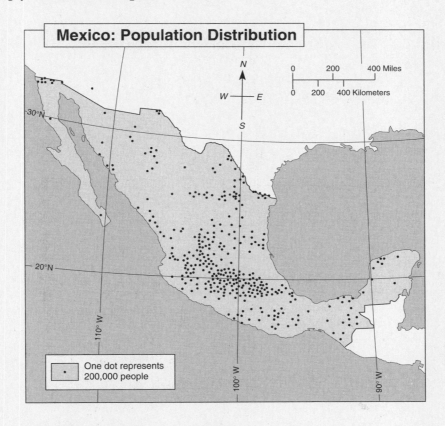

Mexico: Population Distribution

One dot represents 200,000 people

1. What does each dot on the map represent? _____

2. In one or two sentences, describe the population distribution of Mexico as shown on this map.

   _____

   _____

3. What cities lie within the most populated region of Mexico?

   _____

4. What is the difference between a population distribution map and a population density map?

   _____

Map and Globe Skills

Reading a Natural Resources Map

A natural resources map shows what kinds of resources are found in a place and where those resources are located. Some maps use symbols to represent different types of resources; others, like the one below, use letters, such as *G* for gold or *L* for lead.

Directions: Study the map and the map key below. Then, answer the questions that follow. A political map of the United States will help you identify individual states.

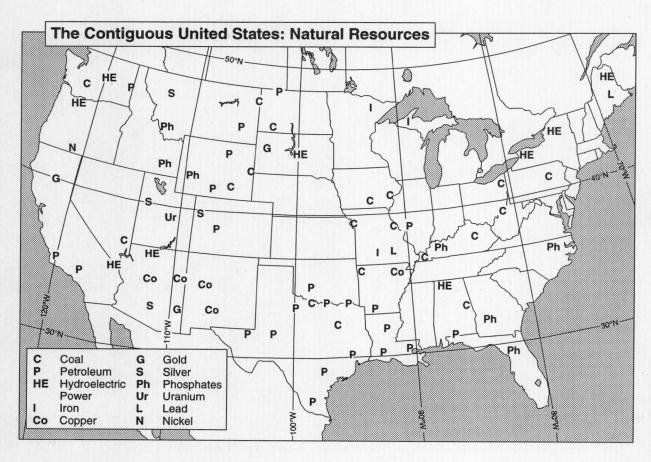

The Contiguous United States: Natural Resources

C	Coal	G	Gold
P	Petroleum	S	Silver
HE	Hydroelectric Power	Ph	Phosphates
		Ur	Uranium
I	Iron	L	Lead
Co	Copper	N	Nickel

1. What is the symbol for coal? _____

2. Which area of the country, according to this map, is least rich in mineral deposits? _____

3. Which of the minerals listed here is not found in the western half of the United States? _____

4. Describe the distribution of major petroleum deposits. _____
_____

5. What landform do all the states with silver deposits have in common? _____

Social Studies Skills Handbook

Map and Globe Skills

Understanding Road Maps

Road maps are important tools for anyone who travels by car. Road maps vary in the colors and symbols they use, but all provide similar basic information. They show the location of cities, the roads that link the cities, and the distances between the cities. Major roads are identified so that you can connect what you see on the map with the road signs that you see en route. The map below shows the road system around Sydney, Australia.

Directions: Study the map and the map key below. Then, answer the questions. Use a separate sheet of paper for your answers.

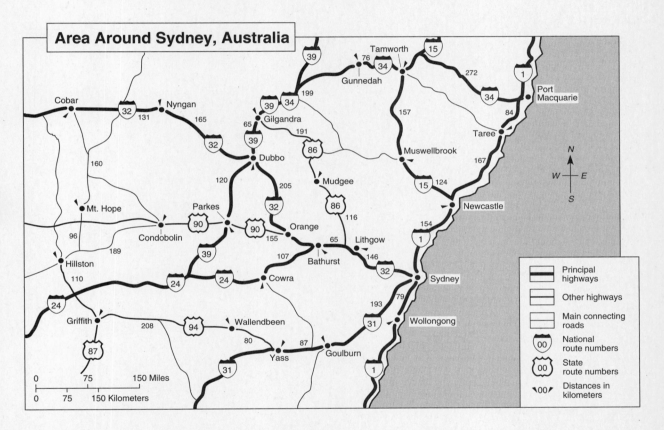

Area Around Sydney, Australia

1. What are the numbers of the three national routes that you could take to reach Sydney?

2. What route would you take to get from Sydney to Cobar, which is in the northwest region of this map?

3. Locate Newcastle on the map. It is north of Sydney. If you traveled northwest from Newcastle on route 15 for 124 kilometers, what town would you reach?

4. Assume you are traveling along state route 94, in the south of the area shown on the map. You are driving east from Griffith to Yass via Wallendbeen. How many kilometers will your journey take?

Map and Globe Skills

Reading a Road Map

Directions: To plan a journey using a road map, you need to understand the symbols used, the scale of the map, and the distances involved. The map below shows the roads in southeastern Tasmania. Study the map and the map key below. Then, answer the questions that follow.

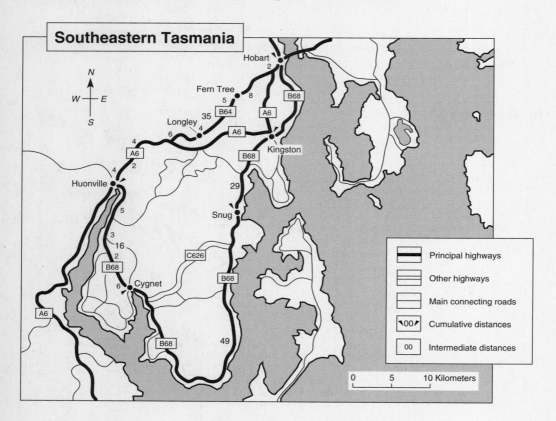

1. What do the heavy black lines on the map represent?

   _____

2. List two towns found along B64.

   _____

3. Suppose you're planning a journey from Hobart to Snug. You're taking the long route there, by way of Huonville and Cygnet, and you'll travel only on principal highways. You'll take the most direct route back, however. Prepare a travel plan listing roads to take and distances involved.

   _____

   _____

   _____

Reading an Ocean Currents Map

An ocean currents map shows the movement of hot and cold ocean waters around the globe. Currents carry warm water from the tropics to the poles and return cold water to the Equator. Because the temperature of the water in these currents heats or cools the winds passing over them, currents affect the temperature of nearby landmasses.

Directions: Study the map and map key below. Then, answer the questions that follow.

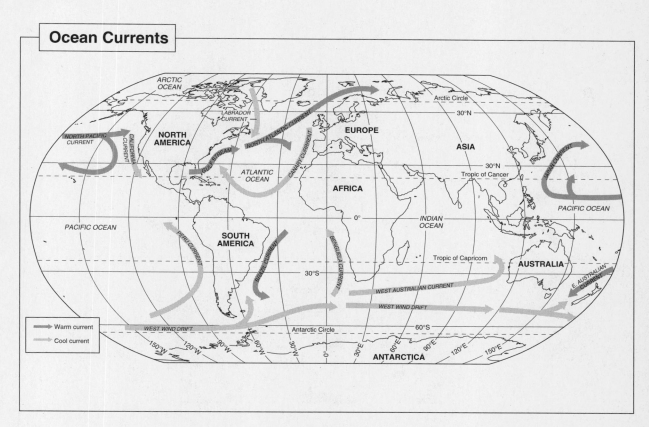

1. Which warm ocean current flows from eastern Canada to northern Europe? _____

   _____

2. Which current brings cool water from the North Pole to the eastern

   Canadian coast? _____

3. In which general direction do the cool currents from Antarctica flow? _____

4. Of the two Australian currents, which is warm and which is cool? _____

   _____

5. Which current has a warming effect on the east coast of the United States? _____

6. Which current has a cooling effect on the west coast of South America? _____

Map and Globe Skills

Reading a Wind Map

A wind map of the world shows the prevailing, or most frequent, wind patterns in different latitudes. Wind patterns begin when light warm air from the Equator rises and flows northward and southward toward the poles. At the same time, cold air from the poles sinks and moves toward the Equator. The rotation of the earth causes the winds to turn or bend. They turn in one direction in the Northern Hemisphere and in another direction in the Southern Hemisphere. The map below shows the patterns and the names of the prevailing winds.

Directions: Study the map and the map key below. Then, answer the questions that follow.

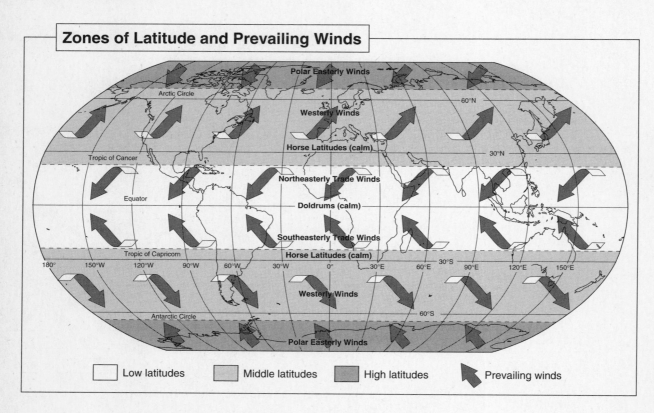

Zones of Latitude and Prevailing Winds

1. Which prevailing winds arise in the polar zones? _____

2. What names are given to the areas of calm? Where are they located? _____
   _____

3. Between which latitudes are the westerlies the prevailing winds? _____

4. Do the westerlies blow from east to west or west to east? _____

5. From which direction do the trade winds blow? _____

Reading a Trade Map

A trade map shows the routes people take to exchange goods with other people. The trade map below shows the sea routes that the ancient Greeks and Romans used. It also indicates the regions that produced the grains that the Greeks and the Romans needed to import.

Directions: Study the map and map key below. Then, answer the questions that follow.

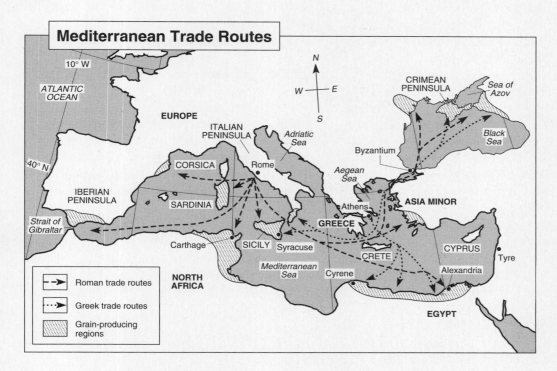

Mediterranean Trade Routes

1. Which two Mediterranean islands provided grain for the Romans?

_____

2. What was the nearest port in North Africa to Rome? _____

3. Which sea did the Greeks have to cross in order to reach the Crimean Peninsula?

_____

4. To which Egyptian port did the Romans sail? _____

5. What was the farthest point west that the Romans sailed? _____

6. What does this map suggest to you about the power and influence of the Greeks and the Romans?

_____

_____

Critical Thinking Skills

Expressing Problems Clearly

To solve a problem, you need to be able to express it clearly. To do that, you need to look at all the relevant facts, identify the main problem, consider all the factors, and decide what can be done about it.

Directions: Read the selection below. Then, answer the questions that follow.

Since the fourteenth century, the Swiss people have protected their mountainside forests, called *Bannwälder.* For hundreds of years, these forests have protected mountain villages and farms from avalanches of snow, falling rocks, and earth slides. But now more than half the trees in the Swiss Alps show signs of damage and decay. Some forests are actually at the point of collapse. One of the main suspects is air pollution, which can injure needles and leaves and change the chemistry of the soil and the plants' ability to absorb nutrients.

Other factors also contribute to tree damage. The forestry practices of the past have created forests containing only one species of tree, all of the same size and age. New trees have not been planted to replace those that have been removed. Then, too, some alpine forests suffer from lack of care; few people want to work in them because the pay is low. When the forests are neglected, bark beetles become a serious problem.

Weakened trees are easily blown over by windstorms. Once just a few trees in a forest collapse, wind erosion enlarges the hole where the trees once stood. The thin layer of soil that surrounds the trees is washed away, making it difficult to plant new trees. Because leaves break the impact of hard rains and tree roots absorb large amounts of rainwater, serious floods have increased in number in sparsely forested areas.

The Swiss have passed some of the strictest pollution-control laws in Europe. They have also begun a program to give the forests emergency care and are planting thousands of tree seedlings to replace those that have died.

1. What is the problem described in the selection?
_____

2. What are some factors that are contributing to the problem?
_____
_____

3. What actions are the Swiss taking to solve the problem?
_____
_____

4. If the problem is not solved, what might the consequences be for people living in small mountain villages?
_____
_____
_____

Identifying the Main Idea

To get the most from your reading, you need to be able to identify the main idea that is being expressed. The main idea is the core of the passage—the message the writer wants you to remember.

Directions: Read the passage below about deforestation in Thailand. Then, answer the questions that follow.

In November 1988, 4 inches (10 cm) of rain fell in 5 days in the mountains of southern Thailand, causing widespread flooding. Thousands of cut logs, left to dry on the mountain slopes, were swept down hillsides by the heavy downpours, crushing entire villages. The flooding and slides killed more than 350 people.

The disaster caused a public outcry that heavy logging had created the deforestation that had caused the soil erosion and water runoff, which resulted in the calamity. In January 1989, in response to public pressure, the government of Thailand banned all commercial logging operations in the country. Before actually ordering the ban, government officials studied satellite photographs that showed that the country's forest cover had declined from 29 percent in 1985 to 19 percent in 1988. At that rate of deforestation, Thailand would have lost half of its forest by 2022.

Alarmed by the ban, Thai timber companies pressured the government to compensate them for their timber losses. To offset the economic impact of the ban, the companies began logging operations in neighboring Laos and Myanmar. The ban was expected to push up the cost of wood in Thailand, probably leading to increased illegal tree harvesting.

Although the ban on logging was an important step in preserving Thailand's forest resources, other threats remained. Rural villagers still harvest forest products for their personal use. In the northern, western, and northeastern regions of the country, it is still common for farmers to clear and burn forests to cultivate the land. The past government policy of allowing landless people to settle on logged forest reserves poses another threat. Today, about five million people inhabit forest reserves.

1. What is the main idea of each paragraph in the passage?

    First paragraph: _____

    _____

    Second paragraph: _____

    _____

    Third paragraph: _____

    _____

    Fourth paragraph: _____

    _____

2. Summarize the main idea of the passage as a whole. _____

    _____

    _____

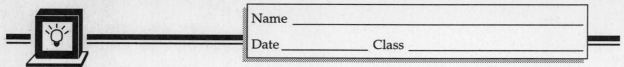
Critical Thinking Skills

Identifying Central Issues

To identify the central issue of a written passage, you need to take the following steps:

1. Find the topic of the passage.

2. Determine the point of view.

3. Look for evidence supporting key statements.

You should then be able to identify and express the central issue.

Directions: As you read the case study, think about the central issue the study addresses. Then, complete the activity that follows.

Case Study: Pudukkupam

Pudukkupam is a fishing village on the east coast of India. For years, a chronic problem for the people living in the village was malaria. Efforts to use the pesticide DDT to kill the mosquitoes that carry the disease were unsuccessful. A few years ago, the people of Pudukkupam participated in an experimental project to test the idea that mosquitoes could be eliminated by destroying their breeding sites and preventing the development of mosquito larvae.

There were several places where malaria-carrying mosquitoes bred. In the villagers' homes, they bred in water-filled pots where coconut husks were soaked to make ropes. Outside, they bred in rice paddies and irrigation pits and in coastal lagoons infested with aquatic algae. Led by officials of a medical research center, the villagers built one large pit to soak coconut husks. They placed a lid of palm leaves over the pit to keep mosquitoes out. They successfully introduced fish into the rice paddies and irrigation pits to eat the mosquito larvae. Finally, they regularly cleared the algae from the lagoons, wiping out still another breeding site.

The results of the experiment were impressive. Not only were no cases of malaria reported in the village for three years, but there were unexpected economic rewards as well. Researchers discovered that the algae in the lagoons could be mixed with cotton waste and made into writing paper. Sales of writing paper as well as sales of mature fish from the rice paddies became profitable sources of revenue for the villagers.

Imagine that you are the director of the Pudukkupam project. You have been asked to write a short report about your project for an international journal. Use the information in the case study as the basis for writing your report. In your report, be sure to include the major purpose and the results of your study. Write your report on the back of this paper or on a separate sheet of paper.

© Prentice-Hall, Inc.

Distinguishing Fact from Opinion

You need to be able to distinguish fact from opinion in order to reach your own conclusions about issues and events. To do that, you need to determine which statements are based on facts that can be proved and which statements express a person's beliefs or feelings.

Directions: Study the statements below about Adolf Hitler. Then, answer the questions that follow.

1 Adolf Hitler was born in Branau, Austria, in 1889.

2 While in jail after an unsuccessful attempt to overthrow the Bavarian government, Hitler wrote *Mein Kampf.*

3 *Mein Kampf* is one of the most fascinating political books ever written.

4 Hitler gave himself the title *Führer* ("Leader") in 1934.

5 Two of Hitler's foreign policy goals were the destruction of the treaty of Versailles and the transformation of Germany into a military power in Europe.

6 If Hitler had not been so egotistical, he would have succeeded in his plans to dominate Europe.

7 Hitler was stubborn; he refused to leave his headquarters in Berlin when the Soviets arrived.

8 Hitler, the most brutal dictator the world has ever known, was responsible for the mass extermination of nearly six million Jews.

1. Which statements are based solely on facts?

    _____

2. What two sources could you use to check these statements to make sure they are true?

    _____

    _____

3. Which statements express opinions?

    _____

4. Which statements, if any, contain both facts and opinions?

    _____

5. Which opinions, if any, are supported by at least one fact?

    _____

    _____

    _____

Critical Thinking Skills

Checking Consistency of Ideas

Ideas are consistent when there is a logical connection between them. Inconsistency occurs when a logical connection between two ideas is missing or when two ideas cannot both be true. To check for consistency of ideas, you need to study viewpoints carefully so that you can confirm that ideas are in agreement with each other.

Directions: Read the following information about oil exploration in the Arctic region. Then, answer the questions that follow.

To meet a growing consumer demand, in the 1970s the United States began to import more oil, an increasing proportion of which came from the Middle East. In 1973, when several Arab nations went to war with Israel and declared an oil embargo against the nations that supported Israel, the United States and most of Western Europe faced an energy crisis. The United States, along with most of the world, faced an energy crisis again in 1990 when Iraq invaded Kuwait.

Many Americans believe that the United States must become less dependent on foreign energy sources. One way to meet this goal is to develop the oil resources that lie within our national borders.

Prudhoe Bay, in the northeast corner of Alaska, is the site of the largest oil field in the United States. No one knows if sufficient quantities of oil will be found there to make exploration and recovery worthwhile. The region is, however, located between known petroleum fields in Canada and the United States. Geologists therefore believe that the petroleum-bearing rock of these known fields is probably present in Prudhoe Bay as well. This suggests to many that the region is the most promising remaining area in the United States for finding large oil fields.

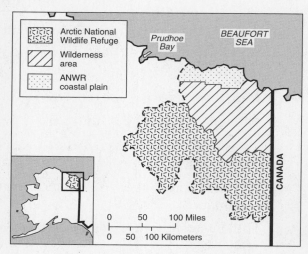

Many Americans, however, are concerned about environmental protection. Prudhoe Bay lies near the western edge of the Arctic National Wildlife Refuge (ANWR), a 19-million-acre wilderness area. The coastal plain that makes up part of the wilderness area is a unique Arctic ecosystem. It is also part of a larger and equally fragile wilderness area that is home to caribou, polar bears, musk oxen, and various species of migrating birds. Oil field technology is likely to damage or destroy the habitats of some or all of these creatures.

1. Why do many Americans want the United States to develop its own oil resources?

_____

2. What is the site of the largest oil field in the United States? _____

3. What is the environmental importance of the Prudhoe Bay area of Alaska? _____

_____

4. What is inconsistent about calling for oil development in Alaska *and* preservation of the environment? _____

5. What might be done to deal with this inconsistency? _____

Distinguishing False from Accurate Images

Images that you have of particular people or places may be based on inaccurate or out-of-date information. To distinguish false from accurate images, you need to identify the main point of new information, evaluate the reliability of the source, and look for supporting evidence. A point of view presented without evidence may be merely someone's opinion.

Directions: The information below is from a report prepared by the World Resources Institute. This not-for-profit research group provides countries with data on the management of natural resources. It also provides developing countries with technical support on environmental projects. First, read the passage. Then, answer the questions that follow. Use a separate sheet of paper for your answers.

The Caribbean is a major oil-producing area, and spilled oil is the area's most widespread pollution problem. An estimated 6.7 percent of total offshore oil production in the region is lost through spills and accidents, and oil is a major pollutant in coastal areas. High levels of petroleum are generally found in Caribbean waters, and windward-exposed coasts are contaminated with tar.

Around large urban areas, sewage threatens Caribbean waters, beaches, and water supplies. Most sewage in the region is discharged untreated into rivers or harbors or is piped to cesspools, where it seeps out to pollute ground water, creating serious water pollution problems. In addition to urban sewage, direct discharge from resort hotels onto swimming beaches can be a health and pollution problem. Although many hotels are equipped with prefabricated treatment plants, the plants are often overloaded or maintained inadequately.

Another major coastal pollution problem is sedimentation. As tropical forests are cleared, the soil erodes and is washed into the sea by heavy rains. Two other sources of sedimentation are agricultural runoff and mining activities, particularly the mining of bauxite. Sediments smother sea grass beds and coral reefs and clog streams. "Red mud," a waste product from bauxite processing, is highly toxic. Fertilizers can cause blooms of algae. When pesticides used in farming reach the ocean, they can be absorbed by fish. One study of ocean pollution uncovered DDT and DDE in the tissue of grouper fish from the Gulf of Mexico and the Caribbean.

Many Caribbean beaches have been severely damaged by recreational activities, and some in Curaçao and Bonaire, off the northern coast of Venezuela, are totally unusable. The most destructive activity affecting beach erosion is mining beach sand. Sand is mined mainly for road-building materials used on the islands. Beach-mining operations on several islands have seriously disturbed coastal and marine ecosystems.

1. What image do most people have of the Caribbean? How does that image of the Caribbean differ from the one described in the passage?

2. Evaluate the reliability of the source of the data presented in the passage.

3. What evidence is presented in the passage to support the conclusion that pollution is a serious problem in the Caribbean?

© Prentice-Hall, Inc.

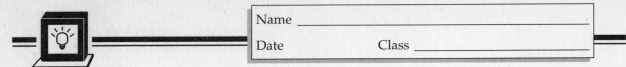

Critical Thinking Skills

Identifying Assumptions

To determine whether a written article is valid, you need to be able to identify and evaluate its assumptions. To do this, read the article carefully, and determine whether the author is presenting a particular point of view. Then, identify the assumptions upon which the article is based, and decide if they are valid or true.

Directions: The passage below describes political and economic changes that took place in Czechoslovakia before it split into two countries in 1993. Read the passage carefully. Then, answer the questions that follow. Use a separate sheet of paper for your answers.

The year 1989 saw the collapse of communism in Czechoslovakia and elsewhere in the region. Ruled by a leadership that was widely regarded by outside observers as one of the most resistant of the East European countries to the changes sparked by Soviet President Mikhail Gorbachev's policies, Czechoslovakia seemed an unlikely candidate to follow Hungary and Poland on the road to radical reform. And yet, once the process of change began, Czechoslovakia took the lead in the effort to restore a multiparty democratic political system and a market economy.

. . . [O]nce the process of change began in Czechoslovakia, the old system was swept away quickly. The "Velvet Revolution," as the mass demonstrations that followed the brutal police attack on peaceful student demonstrators on November 17, 1989, came to be called, led to the resignation of the conservative Communist party leadership . . . and the formation of the country's first non-Communist government in 41 years . . . Free elections . . . legitimized this government and set the stage for the changes needed to consolidate democratic government, to reform the economy and to reorient the country's external economic and political relations . . .

As 1990 draws to a close, the process of change and transformation begun with the dramatic events of late 1989 continues in Czechoslovakia. In the political realm, the transition to post-Communist rule has occurred smoothly. Barring a severe economic crisis or an unanticipated increase in support for extreme nationalist groups, it is likely that the democratic political system that is being recreated will survive the many challenges it faces. Although there are forces in Czechoslovakia that do not support the new order, the country's level of economic development, its Western orientation, its developed social structure and its previous experience with democratic political institutions all bode well for the future of democracy.

The country's standard of living, modest Western debt and trained labor force also provide resources that can be used to support economic reform and buffer its negative effects. . . .

Sharon L. Wolchik, "Czechoslovakia's `Velvet Revolution,'" *Current History,* December 1990.

1. What is the topic of the article?

2. How would you describe the tone of the article?

3. What assumptions does the author make concerning the ease with which Czechoslovakia will change to a democratic political system and a free market economy? Is this assumption stated?

4. Does the author assume that economic forces influence a country's political decisions? Explain.

Recognizing Bias

To evaluate what you are reading, you need to be able to recognize bias. Biased descriptions present only one point of view. To recognize bias, ask yourself if the writer makes assumptions that are not justified. Charlie Pye-Smith is a British writer who realized how biased some history books had been. The selection below is from his book *The Other Nile*, published in 1986.

Directions: Read the selection below. Then, answer the questions that follow.

There was a recent copy of the *Egyptian Gazette* in my hotel room. I skimmed through it . . . and my attention was caught by an item of news which came from one of the gulf emirates [territories governed by an Arabian prince] . . . that the ruler had selected a group of eminent [outstanding] historians to rewrite his country's history. Their task was to rectify [correct] the "errors" made by previous histories. . . .

At first this all struck me as farcical [absurd]. Yet when I thought of the books which I had pored over [studied] as a child, books about Africa and explorers, I realized that this ruler was following in the noble tradition of the Victorian [nineteenth-century English] historians, whose interpretation of the events in Africa was outstanding more for its racial bigotry, its presumption of white superiority, and its [lack of interest] in the fate of Africans, than for any erudition [scholarship] or accuracy in recounting what really happened out here. I grew up thinking of the Nile simply as a geographical conundrum [puzzling problem] . . . and the heroes of my books were men like Baker, Speke, Stanley, Livingstone, and Burton [English explorers of the Nile River and its sources]. It was Speke, as far as my histories were concerned, who had discovered the source of the Nile—no mention was made of the Arabs who for centuries had known where it was (near Lake Victoria), let alone the Africans who actually lived there. This history, written by Europeans and for Europeans, had a certain flavour of romance to it when I was young. Now it bores me profoundly, since the main characters are interesting not for their vision of what might have become in Africa (few had any), but only for their idiosyncrasies [behavioral peculiarities]. . . . [F]or the most part these explorers—there were exceptions like Livingstone—went to Africa for self-aggrandizement [to increase their own power, rank, or honor] and for whatever kudos [praise] they could attract by their adventure.

From *The Other Nile* by Charlie Pye-Smith. Published by Penguin Books Ltd. Copyright © Charlie Pye-Smith 1986.

1. What is the author's criticism of the Victorian historians who wrote books about Africa and the explorers of the Nile?

   _____

   _____

2. How does the author view most of the Europeans who explored the Nile River?

   _____

3. According to Charlie Pye-Smith, why are some historians, such as the Victorian historians he cites, inaccurate in their interpretation of events and unable to recount "what really happened out here"?

   _____

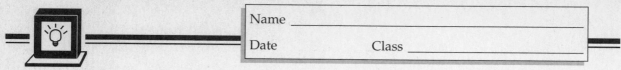

Critical Thinking Skills

Recognizing Ideologies

Ideologies are sets of beliefs that direct the behavior and actions of individuals and societies. Recognizing the ideologies behind an individual or group can help you understand the group and work with it most effectively. When groups with differing ideologies come together without understanding, problems can result.

Directions: The passage below describes colonial efforts to change farming practices in Africa. Read the passage, and then answer the questions that follow.

[T]he small farmers who represent most of Africa's populace are politically mute. And none more so than Africa's women farmers, who grow perhaps 70 percent of the continent's food. . . .

In the pre-colonial era, men and women both worked within the subsistence economy. Women farmed and did household chores, while men focused on hunting and war and helped with clearing land and harvesting. . . . An African woman often lived a life quite separately economically from that of her husband, in which the basic unit was herself and her children. . . . Her husband most often provided her with a hut and some land to farm. She sustained her family by working the land allotted to her and by trading. . . .

[H]owever, with the introduction of cash crops by the colonial administrators, the division of labor shifted further against women. . . . Regarding wives as homemakers and husbands as breadwinners, the Europeans either did not understand or refused to accept the fact that most African farming was done by women. The export crops [that were introduced by the colonists and] grown by men benefited from research, extension advisers, marketing networks, and credit unavailable to the female cultivators of foodstuffs. . . .

Twenty-five years of independence have done little to redress this balance. Because women are even poorer than their husbands and brothers, they are correspondingly less able to make the investments necessary to maintain or increase [crop] yields. . . . An African woman farmer interviewed in 1984 . . . [said]: "This one they call farmer; send in teachers to teach him to farm (while I'm out growing the food); lend him money for tractors and tillers (while I'm out growing the food); promise him fortunes if he'd only raise cotton (while I'm out growing the food). . . . No, I daren't stop working . . . and I won't abandon that thing I was born for—to make sure my children have food in their bellies."

Jennifer Seymour Whitaker, *How Can Africa Survive?* (New York: Council on Foreign Relations Press, 1989), pp. 98, 150-152

1. What was the European ideology, or set of beliefs, about the roles of men and women?

   _____

2. How was this ideology at odds with the traditional division of labor in African society?

   _____

   _____

3. What effect did the ideology of European administrators and introduction of cash crops have on Africa's women farmers?

   _____

   _____

Recognizing Cause and Effect

To understand geography, you need to understand the relationship between cause and effect. A cause is an event or an action that brings about an effect. Remember that an event can have more than one cause and more than one effect. Remember, too, that an event is often both a cause *and* an effect. An effect soon becomes the cause of future events, causing a chain of cause-and-effect relationships.

Directions: The passage below describes how deserts are created and enlarged. As you read the passage, look for cause-and-effect relationships. Then, fill in each missing cause or effect below.

The dryness that causes deserts usually begins at the Equator where warm, moist air rises. As the rising air cools, it sheds its moisture in rain over the tropics and drifts toward the poles. By the time the air reaches about latitudes 15° north and south of the Equator, it begins to descend and warm again, but it is too dry to form clouds and produce rain. This belt of dry air parches the earth, creating a series of deserts around the globe.

Coastal mountains also help to form deserts. When warm, moist ocean air moves inland, it is forced to rise over the mountains. As the air rises, it cools and releases its moisture as rain on the windward slopes of the mountain. By the time the air flows down the other side of the mountain, it is too dry to produce any more rain.

Though deserts are formed by natural conditions, people have contributed to their expansion. More than a third of the world's population depends on wood for heating and cooking. To meet this demand for firewood, people cut down trees in the dry grasslands that rim the deserts. Once the trees are gone, the wind easily carries away the unprotected soil and the land becomes part of the desert.

Animals such as sheep, goats, and cattle also contribute to expansion of desert areas. These animals rely on the grasslands around deserts for their food. However, there are too many animals for the grasses to support. Consequently, the animals overgraze, stripping the lands of their already sparse vegetation and helping to turn them into barren wastes.

1. **Cause:** Dry air at latitudes 15° north and south of the Equator parches the earth.

   Effect: _____

2. **Cause:** Warm, moist air rises at the Equator.

   Effect: _____

3. **Cause:** _____

   Effect: The air that flows down the inland slope of a mountain is dry.

4. **Cause:** People who live around deserts need firewood for cooking and heating.

   Effect: _____

5. **Cause:** Animals overgraze the dry grasslands that rim the desert.

   Effect: _____

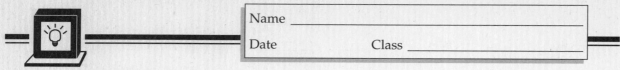
Critical Thinking Skills

Predicting Consequences

You can learn to predict the consequences of events and trends by following certain steps as you read. First, try to gain a clear understanding of the event or the trend. Then consider all the possible consequences, and evaluate which are the most likely to occur. As you think about possible consequences, consider all the groups involved. An event is likely to affect different groups in different ways.

Directions: Apply the steps just described to analyze the passages below. Then, answer the questions that follow.

Passage A   Early Indian nationalism was represented by three main groups, each hostile to the others. The moderate group admired the British and wanted to imitate their educational, social, and political systems. The extremist group, inspired by nationalistic pride in India's Hindu heritage, mistrusted the British, rejected their culture, and doubted that India would ever gain its independence without violence. Indian Muslims, who represented the third group, were a minority population and worried that Muslims would become second-class citizens in India unless constitutional provisions were made to protect their political rights.

Passage B   In 1919 Britain's Parliament gave Indians the right to vote for officials at the local government level, although an appointed governor continued to hold final authority. Most Indians felt these concessions did not go far enough in giving Indians control over their country, and the general reaction was negative. Many Indian radicals called for a violent overthrow of the British government. In response, the British passed the Rowlatt Acts, which gave the government the power to arrest and imprison political agitators without trial. Soon after, a British army officer opened fire on a large group of political demonstrators who had gathered in clear violation of a government order. Nearly 400 Indians were killed and more than 1,000 were wounded in the Amritsar Massacre.

1. What are two possible consequences of the tension among the three groups described in passage A?

    _____

    _____

2. Describe two possible consequences of the Amritsar Massacre for the character of the Indian independence movement.

    _____

    _____

3. Describe two possible consequences of the Amritsar Massacre for British policies toward Indians.

    _____

    _____

Name	
Date	Class

Identifying Alternatives

When looking for solutions to problems, you need to think both of solutions that have worked in the past *and* of possible new solutions. One way to identify a wide variety of alternatives is to brainstorm ideas with others. Everyone should be encouraged to express their ideas no matter how silly they may seem. Even an idea that doesn't quite work on its own may lead to another solution that *is* workable.

In the 1980's, land prices in Japan spiraled upward at a rapid rate. In Tokyo's Ginza shopping district, a patch of ground the size of a dollar bill cost $24,000. Between 1986 and 1990, the price of a modest home increased from $250,000 to $400,000.

Directions: The passage below explains some of the factors that made land prices so high in Japan. As you read, think about what steps the government might have taken to deal with this problem. Then, complete the activity that follows.

For many young, single Japanese, home is a small room in a company dormitory, with a shared bathroom and telephone. Some Japanese companies, especially financial institutions, provide dormitories for their employees, who choose to live there because of the low rent. Rooms cost about $44 a month, far below the $440 to $600 a month that is the usual cost of renting a room in Tokyo. Dormitories are also conveniently located to work, an attractive feature in a city where the average commuting time is 90 minutes.

The cost of housing is extremely high in Japan because of soaring land prices, and many Japanese have given up hope of ever owning a home. According to a recent government survey, the average new apartment of about 625 square feet (58 sq m) in Tokyo costs $600,000, more than 12 times the average income of Tokyo residents. High property costs also make it difficult for foreign businesses to operate in Japan, because they cannot afford to buy land.

Why are property prices in Japan among the highest in the world? Economists maintain that a shortage of land is not the primary reason. They blame Japan's tax laws instead. Current real estate taxes are so low that they encourage individuals and businesses to become land speculators, buying land and holding onto it as it increases in value. As a result, thousands of acres in Tokyo are left idle, serving as an inexpensive way to store wealth.

For years the government has promised to enact new laws to help control increasing land prices. However, it has failed to live up to its promises. One reason is that government policies are strongly influenced by Japanese businesses, which help pay for the campaign expenses of the ruling Liberal Democratic Party.

Form groups of four or five students, and brainstorm ideas that might have been used to solve this problem in Japan's recent history. Think about new laws that could have been introduced, ways people might have been persuaded to change their practices, and political reforms that might have been instituted. Select one group member to write down all of your group's ideas and another to present them to the class. Compare your group's findings with those of other groups.

© Prentice-Hall, Inc.

Critical Thinking Skills

Drawing Conclusions

Drawing conclusions means figuring out information that is suggested but not stated directly. To do this, you must first study carefully the facts and ideas that are presented. Then, to check your understanding, try to summarize the information provided. Finally, consider whether you can draw any valid conclusions from what you have seen or read. Remember that your conclusions should be based on both the facts presented and good reasoning skills.

Directions: The map below shows the location of active volcanoes and earthquake zones. Study the map, and then answer the questions that follow.

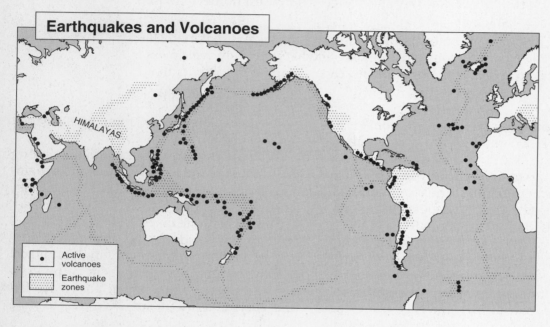

1. What is the relationship between the location of active volcanoes and the location of earthquake zones?

   _____

   _____

2. Compare this map with a map in your textbook or atlas that shows the boundaries of the different tectonic plates. What can you conclude about the relationship between earthquake zones and plate boundaries?

   _____

   _____

3. Although there is no volcanic activity shown on the map for the region of the Himalayas, the area is shaded to show an earthquake zone. Why would you expect earthquakes to occur there?

   _____

   _____

Name _____

Date _____ Class _____

Reading a Bar Graph

A bar graph enables you to compare quantities of different things. Each bar stands for an amount of something. The longer the bar, the more there is of that item. The bar graph below compares exports and imports for four Mediterranean countries. You can use the scale on the left of the bar graph to estimate approximate quantities.

Directions: Study the bar graph below, and answer the questions that follow. Then, draw your own bar graph. Use a separate sheet of paper for your answers.

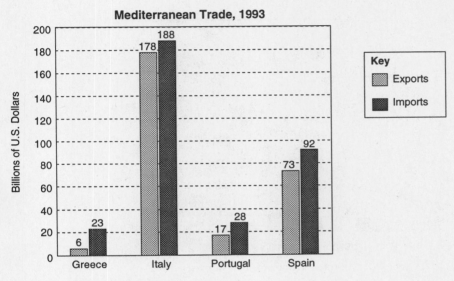

Source: *World Almanac and Book of Facts, 1996.*

1. Which country imported the most goods in 1993?

2. Which country exported the fewest goods in 1993?

3. Roughly how much did Portugal import and how much did it export in 1993?

4. Which country shows the greatest difference between the amount it imported and the amount it exported?

5. Draw a bar graph that compares average January and July temperatures in four cities. The scale on the left should start at 0°F and go to 100°F. The four cities, with their temperatures, are as follows:

City		January		July	
Athens, Greece	January:	48°	July:	81°
Toronto, Canada	January:	23°	July:	69°
Auckland, New Zealand	January:	66°	July:	51°
Buenos Aires, Argentina	January:	74°	July:	50°

   Write one or two sentences describing a conclusion that can be drawn from this graph.

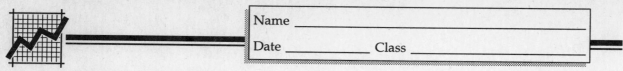

Graph and Chart Skills

Reading a Line Graph

A line graph shows changes that take place over time. It has two axes. One measures time and the other measures quantity. The line graph below shows world population growth over a 350-year period. Different colors of shading indicate growth for developed and developing regions.

Directions: Study the line graph below, and answer the questions that follow. Then, draw your own line graph. Use a separate sheet of paper for your answers.

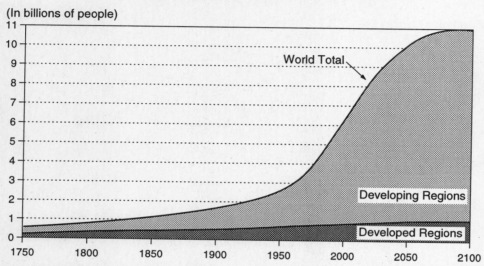

World Population Growth, 1750–2100

Source: World Resources Institute/United Nations Environmental Programme, *World Resources 1992-93.*

1. In which century was the rate of population growth greater—in the 1800s or the 1900s?

2. What is the total world population expected to be by the year 2100?

3. What was the world's population in 1950?

4. When was the world's population evenly divided between developed and developing regions?

5. What probably accounts for the greater increase in population in developing regions than in developed regions?

6. On a separate sheet, draw a line graph that shows U.S. imports and exports, in billions of dollars, from 1970 to 1994. The scale at the left should start at 0 and go to 700, using divisions of 100. The years go along the bottom. Use the following figures:

Year	1970	1975	1980	1985	1990	1995
Imports	40	99	245	345	495	743
Exports	43	108	221	213	394	584

What does your completed line graph tell you about imports and exports over that period?

Name _____

Date _____ Class _____

Reading a Circle Graph

A circle graph enables you to compare parts with a whole. The complete circle represents all of something. Each section represents a percentage of the whole. Together, the sections add up to 100 percent. The circle graph below shows how the world's population is divided among different religions.

Directions: Study the circle graph, and answer the questions that follow. Then, draw your own circle graph.

Estimated Religious Population of the World

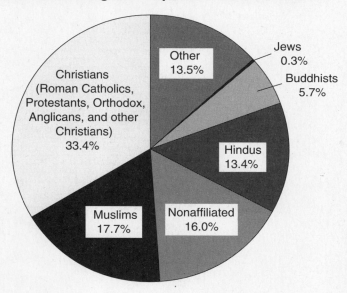

1. What percentage of the world's population is Muslim? _____

2. What percentage is Jewish? _____

3. Which religious group has the most members? _____

4. Which religious group is the second largest in the world? _____

5. How many times greater than the Muslim population is the Christian population?

_____

6. On a separate sheet, draw a circle graph that shows how the world's population is divided by region. Use the following figures:

   Africa 12.5%; North America 5%; Latin America and the Caribbean 8%; Asia 61%; Europe 13%; Oceania 0.5%.

   What does your circle graph tell you about the world's population distribution?

_____

_____

Graph and Chart Skills

Reading a Diagram

A diagram is a drawing that shows objects in ways they would not normally be seen. The purpose of a diagram is to help you see at a glance what something is like or how it works. The diagram below shows various landforms and bodies of water.

Directions: Study the diagram below. Then, answer the questions that follow.

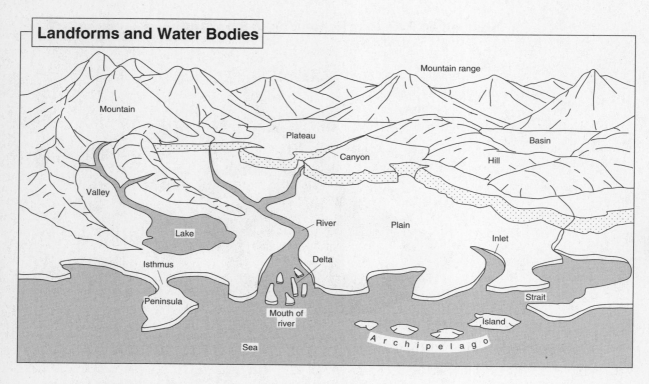

Landforms and Water Bodies

1. What is the difference between a strait and an inlet?

   _____

   _____

2. What is the name given to a land area almost entirely surrounded by water? _____

3. What is an archipelago? _____

4. What is the difference between mountains and hills? _____

   _____

5. What is an isthmus? _____

   _____

6. How can a diagram like this one help make written material more understandable?

   _____

© Prentice-Hall, Inc.

Social Studies Skills Handbook

Reading a Flowchart

A flowchart is a visual guide to a process. It shows the steps in the process and the sequence of those steps. It helps you visualize and remember the ways items are produced. Some flowcharts are illustrated. Others use words to explain the process. The flowchart below shows the steps involved in producing tea.

Directions: Study the flowchart below, and answer the questions that follow. Then, make your own flowchart.

How Tea Is Produced

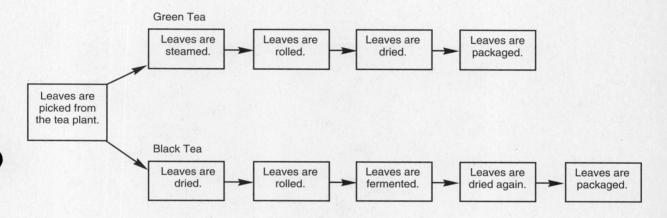

1. What does the flowchart show? _____
   _____

2. What advantage does a flowchart have over a text description? _____
   _____

3. Suggest ways that this flowchart might be illustrated for greater visual impact.
   _____
   _____

4. Draw a flowchart to illustrate one of the following processes (or choose your own):

   How corn is grown and processed into canned or frozen corn

   How wheat becomes bread

   How sugar cane is processed into refined sugar

   Use library resources to do your research. Illustrate your flowchart if you wish.

Graph and Chart Skills

Analyzing a Photograph

The photographs in your textbook help you understand what you are reading. They enable you to visualize landscapes, dwellings, and other features of places that are unfamiliar to you. If you were studying East Asia, for example, you might read about the terracing that is needed to make the land suitable for growing crops. The photograph below shows you at a glance what is meant by terracing.

To analyze a photograph, you need to examine it carefully and observe the details. Look at the overall content of the photograph first, and ask yourself what the photographer intended to show. Then, look at the details. What can you learn about the landscape, the people, the climate, the way of life?

Directions: Study the photograph below of terracing in Bali, an island in Indonesia. Then, answer the questions.

1. What is the overall subject of the photograph?

   _____

2. Using what you see in the photo, describe terracing.

   _____

3. Why would terracing be necessary for farming in this region?

   _____

4. What does the photo tell you about the availability of land for farming in Bali?

   _____

Analyzing Art

Drawings, paintings, and other works of art often provide insights into the geography, history, and culture of a place. Works of art that show scenes from a particular era provide valuable clues to the way people lived at that time.

To analyze a work of art, you need to examine it carefully and observe the details. Ask yourself questions. What is the overall content of the piece? If people are shown, what are they doing? What are they wearing? What tools are they using? What does the piece of art tell you about the geography, history, or culture of the place?

Directions: The picture below is titled *Home in the Wilderness.* It is one of many prints produced by the famous lithographers Currier and Ives. Their works provide a record of American life in the 19th century. Study the picture. Then, answer the questions.

"Home in the Wilderness"/Currier & Ives/Superstock

1. What general impression of pioneer life does the picture give?

   _____

2. What did the pioneers in the picture use to build their home?

   _____

3. Where did their building materials probably come from?

   _____

4. Based on your study of the picture, what tools do you think were most essential for survival in this kind of home?

   _____

5. What clues does the picture offer about what the family ate and how they kept warm?

   _____

Analyzing a Political Cartoon

Political cartoons are drawings that express a point of view. They generally show public figures, political events, or social or economic situations. The cartoonist may use symbols, labels, captions, or exaggeration to make a point.

To analyze a political cartoon, you need to examine it carefully and ask yourself what is happening in the cartoon. Who or what do the characters represent? What symbols are used? What do the labels mean? By studying all the clues, you can identify the point the cartoonist is making.

Directions: Study the political cartoon below, and then answer the questions.

Gary Brookins, 1994 *Richmond Times-Dispatch*. Reprinted by permission of Gary Brookins.

1. Who or what does the lifeguard represent?

   _____

2. What clues helped you identify the lifeguard?

   _____

3. Who or what do the people in the water represent?

   _____

4. Why is the lifeguard perplexed?

   _____

5. What point is the cartoonist making?

   _____

Graph and Chart Skills

Reading a Time Line

A time line shows the order in which events occur and the length of time between them. The time line below shows events in the United Kingdom that were significant to the division of Ireland.

Directions: Study the time line, and answer the questions that follow. Then, draw your own time line.

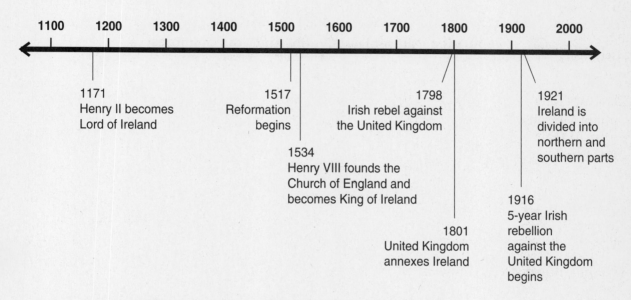

1. When did the Reformation begin? _____

2. How many years after that did Henry VIII establish the Church of England?

   _____

3. How many years passed between the United Kingdom's annexation of

   Ireland and the division of Ireland into two parts? _____

4. What event on the time line led to the division of Ireland into two parts?

   _____

   _____

5. On a separate sheet, draw a time line to illustrate significant events in the history of space exploration. Start with 1961, the year the first human flew in space, and extend the time line to the present day. Use an almanac to find dates and events. Then, select the most significant ones for your time line.

   What does your time line tell you about space exploration?

   _____

   _____

Graph and Chart Skills

Reading a Table

A table presents information in columns (up and down) and rows (across). It allows you to make comparisons and to analyze the information presented. A table is an efficient way of presenting information that lends itself to analysis. The table below presents population data for four countries in Central America.

Directions: Study the table, and then answer the questions that follow.

Population Data for Four Central American Countries				
	Costa Rica	**Panama**	**Honduras**	**Guatemala**
Literacy Rate	93%	88%	73%	55%
Infant Mortality Rate (per 1,000 births)	10	16	43	52
Life Expectancy				
Males	76	73	66	62
Females	80	78	71	68
Workers in Agriculture	27%	27%	62%	60%

Source: *World Almanac and Book of Facts, 1996.*

1. What information is shown in the table?

   _____

2. What are the infant mortality rates in Honduras and Guatemala?

   _____

3. In what way are the life expectancy data for all countries shown similar?

   _____

   _____

4. What relationship between literacy rate and infant mortality rate does this table suggest?

   _____

   _____

5. Identify another relationship from studying the data in the table.

   _____

   _____

6. Which country shown has the highest standard of living? Give reasons for your choice.

   _____

   _____

Mean, Median, and Mode

Statistics are often used in the social sciences to describe a pattern or to make comparisons. The mean, the median, and the mode are three different statistical measures that can be used to describe a group. Each measure provides an approximate central figure so that details about all the group members need not be given.

Directions: Read the following definitions and examples, and study the information about hotels on islands. Then, apply what you have learned to answer the questions.

Mode. The mode is the *most common* value in a group. To find the mode for the age of students in your class, write down the age of each student in years and months. The age that occurs most frequently on your list is the mode.

Mean. The mean is the *average* measure. To find the mean age of students in your class, express each person's age in years and months. Add the ages, and divide by the number of students. The mean usually falls somewhere in the middle of the group.

Median. The median is the exact *middle* value. To find the median age of your class, take the list of students, and put them in order from oldest to youngest or vice versa. An odd number of students would mean there was a "middle" name in the list: that person's age would be the median age. For an even number, the median would be the point halfway between the two "middle" people: 50 percent would be older than the median; 50 percent would be younger.

The list below shows the number of hotels per island in a Pacific archipelago. There are 10 islands and 30 hotels distributed in the following way:

- 1 island has 1 hotel
- 4 islands have 2 hotels
- 1 island has 3 hotels
- 2 islands have 4 hotels
- 2 islands have 5 hotels

1. What is the mode for the number of hotels per island? _____

2. What is the mean number of hotels per island? _____

3. What is the median number of hotels per island? _____

4. Which of the three measures most fairly describes how many hotels a visitor can expect to find on a typical island in the archipelago? Why?

_____

_____

5. Which of the measures gives the best idea of how easily a visitor would get a hotel room somewhere in the archipelago? Why?

_____

_____

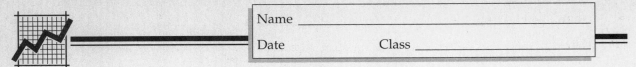

Graph and Chart Skills

Analyzing Statistics

Social scientists use many different kinds of statistics to describe the characteristics of a region or a country. Such statistics are efficient ways of providing information, and they enable you to make quick comparisons. Some of the most commonly used statistics are described below.

Directions: Study the definitions, and then complete the activities.

Birthrate. This rate reflects the number of live births each year for each 1,000 people. A birthrate of 36 means that for every 1,000 people, 36 babies are born each year.

Death Rate. This rate means the number of deaths each year for every 1,000 people.

Rate of Natural Increase. This number tells the rate by which a population is growing: the birthrate minus the death rate, expressed as a percentage.

Infant Mortality Rate. This rate shows the number of infants out of every 1,000 born who die before their first birthday.

Life Expectancy. This figure is the average number of years a person is expected to live. Because men and women have different life expectancies, figures for both genders are often provided.

Literacy Rate. This rate is usually defined as the ability to read and write at the lower elementary school level. It is sometimes defined as the ability to read instructions necessary for a job.

Gross National Product (GNP). This number represents the total value of goods and services produced in a year.

Per Capita GNP. To find this figure, gross national product is divided by the country's population. This figure shows what each person's income would be if the country's income were divided equally. That is not usually the case.

1. Choose three countries that interest you, and find the statistics for each, as listed above. You will find the statistics you need in an almanac.

2. Prepare a table that will enable you to compare the statistics you find.

3. Write a brief description of your findings on the lines below.

_____

_____

_____

_____

_____

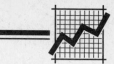
Name _____

Date _____ Class _____

Reading a Climate Graph

A climate graph consists of a line graph and a bar graph that provide information on temperature and precipitation. The line on the graph below shows average temperature in degrees Fahrenheit. The scale for the line graph is on the left. The bars show average precipitation in inches. The scale for the bars is on the right. Temperature and precipitation are given for each month of the year. Letters representing each month appear along the bottom of the graph. This climate graph shows temperature and precipitation for Mumbai (Bombay), India.

Directions: Study the climate graph. Then, answer the questions that follow.

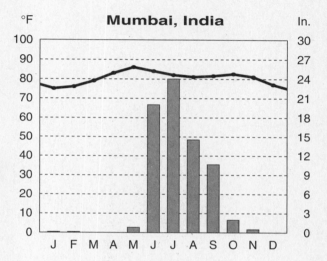

1. What information is presented in the climate graph?

   _____

   _____

2. Which is the rainiest month in Mumbai? _____

3. During which months does Mumbai receive less than 3 inches of rain? _____

   _____

4. During which months does Mumbai receive more than 12 inches of rain? _____

   _____

5. How would you describe the temperature pattern of Mumbai? _____

   _____

6. Do you think the temperatures in Mumbai affect the amount of rainfall? Why
   or why not? _____

   _____

Graph and Chart Skills

Comparing Climate Graphs

Climate graphs enable you to compare climates in different cities. The climate graphs below show the different climate patterns of Seattle, New Delhi, and Paris.

Directions: Study the climate graphs, and answer the questions that follow.

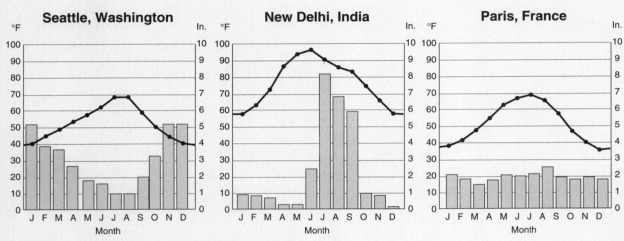

Line graphs show temperature. Bar graphs show precipitation.

A. Temperature

1. Which city has the greatest annual range of temperatures? _____

2. What is the warmest month in New Delhi? _____

3. What are the two coolest months in Seattle? _____

B. Precipitation

4. What is the rainiest month in New Delhi? _____

5. Approximately how many inches of rain fall in that month? _____

6. In which city is precipitation most even throughout the year? _____

7. Which city has the highest total precipitation? _____

C. Comparing climates

8. Which city has the most variable climate? _____

9. Describe the climate of Paris.

_____

_____

_____

_____

Name _____

Date _____ Class _____

Reading a Cartogram

A cartogram is a combination of a graph and a map. The cartogram on the right below shows the countries of Asia and Australia. The size of each country in the cartogram is determined by the size of its gross national product (GNP). The political map on the left shows the accurate land area of each country.

Directions: Compare the cartogram and the political map below. Then, answer the questions that follow.

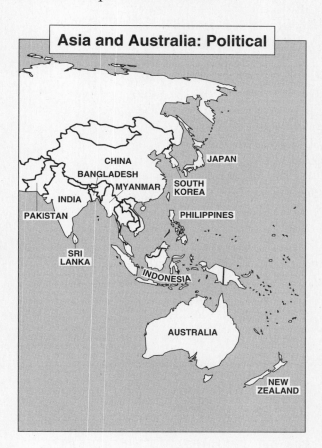

Asia and Australia: Political

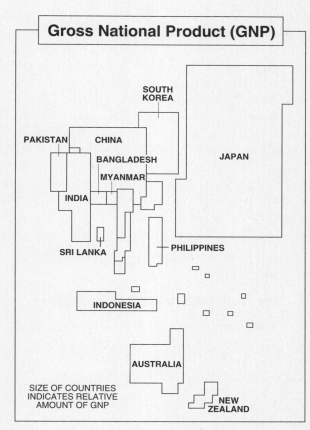

Gross National Product (GNP)

SIZE OF COUNTRIES INDICATES RELATIVE AMOUNT OF GNP

1. What does the cartogram tell you about Japan?

_____

2. Which country has the larger GNP, Indonesia or Sri Lanka? _____

3. What do the relative sizes of Australia and New Zealand on both maps tell you about each country's GNP? _____

4. Compare the size of South Korea on the two maps. What does this comparison tell you?

_____

5. How does China's GNP compare with that of Japan? _____

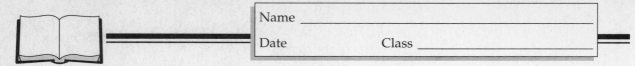
Reading and Writing Skills

Previewing the Headings and the Pictures

Reading a textbook is different from reading a novel or a play. Textbooks are organized to help you find, use, and remember information as easily as possible. Since textbooks are set up in a special way to help you, you need to read them in a special way to take advantage of their organization. You should begin by previewing the headings and the pictures.

The main signposts in your textbooks are the unit titles and the chapter titles. They help you pinpoint what you are reading about and what comes next. When you are assigned a new chapter, the first thing you should do is to read the chapter title. It tells you in a few words what the rest of your reading will be about.

Next, look at the section titles and the titles of the subsections. How are the section topics related to the chapter title? How are the sections related to each other? Finally, look at the photos and other illustrations and read the captions. What do they tell you about the chapter content?

Previewing a chapter in this way is like studying a map when you plan a long road trip. It gives you an idea of where you are going and what you will encounter on the way. By previewing the chapter, you learn what subjects are covered and in what sequence. Previewing helps you determine whether questions you have as you read the early part of the chapter will be answered for you later in the chapter.

Directions: Select a chapter in your textbook that you have not yet read. Preview the headings and the pictures as outlined above. Then, answer the questions below.

1. What is the title of the unit in which the chapter is located? _____

2. What is the title of the chapter? _____

3. What is the title of the first section in the chapter? _____

4. What types of special features are included in the chapter? _____

   _____

5. What topics do the features cover? _____

6. How many sections does the chapter have? _____

7. What do the illustrations in the first section show? _____

   _____

8. Briefly explain what you have learned from previewing the chapter in this way.

   _____

   _____

   _____

   _____

Giving Yourself a Purpose for Reading

You'll get more out of your reading if you have a purpose—one or more goals—in mind when you begin reading a new chapter. Your overall purpose is, of course, to learn and understand the content of the chapter. However, you can break that down into smaller goals that will help you stay focused.

Imagine, for example, that in previewing a chapter on North Africa you see a photo of the Sahara and read a caption saying that the desert is spreading southward. One of your goals in reading the chapter might be to find out why the desert is spreading south, what that means to the people who live in the region, and what, if anything, can be done about it.

Previewing a chapter will raise several questions in your mind that will help you set goals for your reading. You can also study the main ideas or the objectives at the beginning of the chapter. These will help you identify the core content of the chapter and set goals for understanding it.

The main advantage of giving yourself a purpose for reading is that you stay actively involved. By looking for answers to your questions and by searching for the information you need, you are more likely to understand and remember what you read.

Directions: Select a chapter in your textbook that you have not yet read. Then, answer the following questions.

1. Examine the headings and the illustrations. What questions do they raise in your mind? Complete the following sentence, including each question raised in your mind.

   When I read this chapter, I shall look for answers to the following questions:

   _____

   _____

   _____

   _____

2. Now look at the main ideas or objectives at the beginning of the chapter. What questions do they raise in your mind?

   _____

   _____

   _____

3. Summarize your overall purpose for reading the chapter.

   _____

   _____

   _____

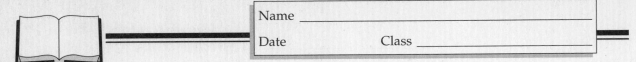

Reading and Writing Skills

Asking Questions While You Read

Asking questions while you read keeps you actively engaged in the reading process. Imagine, for example, that you read that 99 percent of Egypt's people live in the Nile River valley and the Nile delta. You might ask: "Why do they all live there?" "How do they support themselves?" "What are the living conditions like?" Asking questions like those will hold your interest as you look for the answers. Some of your questions will be answered in the chapter. Others may require you to think back to what you have already learned and draw some logical conclusions.

Questions that compare the content of one section with that of another are helpful too. For example, you might ask yourself, "How are Egypt and Libya similar, and how are they different?"

Keep the words *what, why, when, how, where,* and *who* in mind as you are reading. Whenever a question comes to mind, jot it down.

Directions: Select a chapter in your textbook that you have not yet read. Read it carefully now, keeping in mind the question words listed above. Use the spaces below to write the questions that come to mind as you read.

_____

_____

_____

_____

_____

_____

_____

_____

_____

_____

_____

_____

_____

_____

_____

_____

_____

_____

_____

_____

Connecting Content to What You Already Know

The information in your social studies textbook can sometimes seem over-whelming. You learn many facts about history and about many different regions and countries. You'll find the task much easier if you use what you already know to help you understand what you are reading. By applying this active reading technique, you stay involved and are more likely to remember what you read.

Here's an example. In an early lesson, you learned about rivers and deltas. You learned that the sediment that rivers deposit on floodplains and at deltas is good for growing crops. You also learned that rivers are important transportation routes. Now, you are studying the geography of Egypt. You learn that most of Egypt's population lives along the banks of the Nile or in the Nile delta. By connecting what you have already learned about rivers with what you are reading about the Nile, you build your understanding of Egypt's geography.

Directions: Choose a chapter in your textbook that focuses on a region. As you read through the chapter, make a conscious effort to connect the content of the chapter to what you already know. As you approach each topic, review your current knowledge of the subject. On the lines below, explain what you were able to recall for the topics given. Use a separate sheet of paper if you need more space.

Chapter title: _____

What I already knew about the region's . . .

History: _____

_____

Location: _____

_____

Climate: _____

_____

Terrain: _____

_____

People: _____

_____

Economy: _____

_____

Agriculture: _____

_____

Recent events: _____

_____

Reading and Writing Skills

Predicting What You Will Find Out

Predicting what you think you will find out as you read a chapter is another active reading technique. It's a way of applying what you already know to the topic of the chapter. It's also a way of applying what you are learning as you learn it. You might predict how one fact, such as the climate, might affect another fact, such as the kinds of crops grown or the kinds of homes people have. By saying to yourself "I'm sure I'll find out that . . ." as you read through a chapter, you'll stay alert as you look for proof that you are right.

Here's an example. In the beginning of a chapter on Australia, you learn that the country has little water and that much of it is an arid plain. From this information, you can predict that few people live in much of Australia. Similarly, if you study a climate map of Australia, you'll be able to predict where most Australians live: on the eastern coast where the climate is moist and mild. What prediction would you make about Australia's culture if you read that the majority of its people are of British origin?

Directions: Choose a chapter in your textbook that you have not yet read. As you read each important fact, try to make a prediction. What effect on other aspects of the region might that fact have? Why is it significant? Use the lines below, and a separate sheet if you need it, to write your predictions as you read through the chapter.

Chapter title: _____

What I expect to find out:

_____

_____

_____

_____

_____

_____

_____

_____

_____

_____

_____

_____

_____

_____

Visualizing What Things Look Like

As you read your textbook, try to visualize what a place looks like. In this way, you'll build a mental image that will help you remember what you have read. You can use this technique when you read about historical events, climate, physical geography, agriculture, industry, and many other topics.

Here are some examples. As you read about the monsoon rains in India, visualize what the rain looks like, what it sounds like, and how it feels on your skin. As you read about the physical geography of Mexico, visualize the mountain ranges, the plateau, and the coastal plains. As you read about rice growing in Southeast Asia, build a mental image of the flooded paddies and of the laborers bending to plant or harvest the crop. When you learn about the Midwest of the United States, visualize the fields of golden wheat, the combine harvesters, and the tall grain silos.

Directions: Choose a chapter in your textbook. Focus your attention on visualizing what things look like as you read about them. Use the lines below to describe the images that came to mind as you followed these directions.

Chapter title: _____

Images that I visualized as I read about . . .

Topic: _____

Visual image: _____

Topic: _____

Visual Image: _____

Topic: _____

Visual Image: _____

Topic: _____

Visual Image: _____

Topic: _____

Visual Image: _____

Topic: _____

Visual Image: _____

Topic: _____

Visual Image: _____

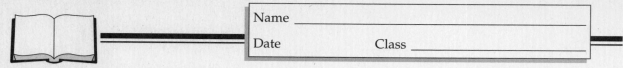
Reading and Writing Skills

Determining If You Understood What You Read

Textbooks are designed to help you make sure you have understood what you read. They do this in a number of ways. Here are brief descriptions of the main methods.

Section Reviews. Most textbooks have questions at the end of or throughout each section within a chapter. These questions generally focus on new vocabulary and on main ideas. Some section reviews include critical thinking questions. These questions go beyond what is in the text and ask you to use your judgment.

Chapter Reviews. Chapter reviews generally include review questions that ask about the content of the chapter, vocabulary questions that test your understanding of key vocabulary terms, and critical thinking questions. Some textbooks also have map exercises, activities, and projects in the chapter reviews.

Caption Questions. To help make sure you have understood a map or a photo, many textbooks include a question with the caption.

Feature Questions. Special features in the text may be followed by review questions or critical thinking questions.

Directions: Analyze your textbook to determine what methods it uses to help you check your understanding. Choose a representative chapter, and then answer the questions below.

1. Title of textbook: _____

2. Does the textbook have section reviews? _____

   If so, describe the questions found in the section reviews. _____

   _____

3. What kinds of questions do the chapter reviews have? _____

   _____

   _____

4. What other kinds of questions does your textbook have? _____

   _____

5. Which questions help you determine if you understood the new vocabulary in the chapter?

   _____

6. Which questions help you determine if you understood the facts in the chapter?

   _____

7. Which questions challenge you to think beyond what you have read in the chapter?

   _____

   _____

Demonstrating What You Know

Projects and activities provide opportunities for you to demonstrate what you know. Many textbooks include project suggestions. In addition, your teacher may suggest projects, or you may have your own ideas. The goal of these projects is to show that you have understood the content of a chapter. Typical methods for demonstrating what you know are listed below:

- Draw a map.
- Draw a picture.
- Draw a diagram.
- Prepare a collage.
- Make a presentation.
- Participate in a debate.
- Write a report.

- Write a story.
- Write a poem.
- Write a letter.
- Prepare a tape recording.
- Make a video.
- Make a flowchart.
- Create a poster.

Directions: Choose a chapter in your textbook that you have already read. Scan it or reread it to remind yourself of the chapter content. Then, think of three ways you could demonstrate what you know about the subject of the chapter. Write your ideas on the lines below, explaining how you would prepare and present each project. You may choose any of the project types listed above, or you can come up with your own project ideas.

Chapter title: _____

Here are three ways I can demonstrate what I know about

1. _____
    _____
    _____
    _____
    _____

2. _____
    _____
    _____
    _____
    _____

3. _____
    _____
    _____
    _____
    _____

Reading and Writing Skills

Learning More About a Topic

Your textbook contains a great deal of information. Sometimes, however, you need more information than the textbook provides.

Imagine, for example, that you've decided to write a report on sheep farming in New Zealand. You need statistics on the number and varieties of sheep in New Zealand and information about wool gathering and processing—information that your textbook does not have. Or imagine that you've decided to make a flowchart showing how oil in Saudi Arabia is extracted, processed, and shipped to the United States. For this, you need technical information and illustrations that are not available in your textbook.

How do you go about learning more about such topics? The first place to start is the library. The library's catalogs and indexes can direct you to the books and articles you need. Encyclopedias may also be helpful. If you have access to the Internet, you can search electronically for information as well. However, first you need to identify just what it is you need to look for. What kind of statistics do you need? What kind of details are relevant to your project? By thinking carefully about what you want, you can focus your search for information.

Directions: Write down three projects your teacher might assign you in this course. What information would you need to gather in order to do the projects? Where would you find that information? On the lines below, list the topics you would need to research. Then, describe how you would go about carrying out the research.

Project 1. _____

_____

_____

_____

Project 2. _____

_____

_____

_____

Project 3. _____

_____

_____

_____

Overview: The Writing Process

The writing process is the name for a useful system to follow when writing a paper. The process is divided into four stages: prewriting, drafting, revising, and presenting. You practice different skills and undertake different activities at each of these stages.

Directions: Read the descriptions of each stage in the writing process, and then answer the questions.

Prewriting. The object of this stage is to prepare everything you will need when you start writing. During this stage, you choose a topic and define its scope. You then use a variety of sources to gather information on your subject, keeping careful records of where you find your data. Finally, you should put your notes in order to create an outline, or a plan, for writing.

Drafting (Writing). In this stage, you use your outline and your notes to prepare a first version of your paper. You provide an introduction and then present your information and conclusions. You make generalizations and provide your reader with supporting material for those generalizations. You also select visuals and prepare your footnotes and bibliography during this stage.

Revising. In this stage, you carefully review your work. You check for content: Have you included all the necessary information? You check for clarity: Have you explained everything clearly? You check for style: Are your ideas clearly connected? Is the writing smooth? Finally, you check for accuracy: Are grammar, spelling, and punctuation all correct?

Presenting. This final stage involves preparing the final form of your report. Preparing a neat, attractive product shows pride in your work and respect for yourself and for your reader.

1. What are the four stages of the writing process? _____
   _____

2. Summarize what you do during the prewriting stage. _____
   _____

3. During which stage do you choose visuals and prepare footnotes and bibliography?
   _____

4. What do you check for during the revising stage? _____
   _____

5. What, do you think, are the advantages of following the steps of the writing process?
   _____
   _____
   _____

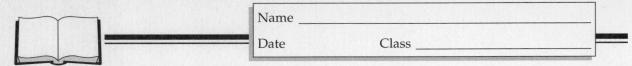
Reading and Writing Skills

Prewriting: Choosing a Topic

When you write in school, your topic may be assigned to you, or you may choose your own topic within guidelines set by your teacher. In either case, examine the topic carefully. You need to define what it will include—which also involves deciding what it will *not* include.

Directions: Read the guidelines below for choosing a topic. Then, complete the activities that follow.

Whether you are writing a paragraph, an essay, or a report, your first step is to choose and then limit your topic. The following guidelines should start you on your way to a successful piece of writing:

- Select a topic you find interesting. A writer is more likely to write knowledgeably and well about a subject that interests him or her.

- Consider how much information is available on the topic. If you discover partway through your task that you do not have enough data to write a paper of the assigned length, you will have wasted valuable time.

- Narrow your topic to one you can easily write about in the given amount of time and in the given length. Too broad a subject may become so general that your paper loses its purpose.

For example, Andrew must write a descriptive paragraph about a favorite place in his community. His favorite place is the nature park, but he knows he cannot do it justice in one paragraph. So he limits his topic and writes a colorful description of his favorite hiking trail along Muskrat Creek.

Study the groups of topics below. In each group, which topic is best suited to a one-page essay? Circle the letter.

1. **a.** The History of Mapmaking
   b. What Is a Landsat Image?
   c. The North American Landscape

2. **a.** Night Sounds in the Rain Forest
   b. Explorers of the Brazilian Rain Forest
   c. Tourist Attractions in Brazil

3. **a.** The People and Culture of France
   b. France During World War I
   c. The Relative Location of France

4. **a.** Southwest Asia
   b. The Physical Geography of Iraq
   c. Religion in Southwest Asia

Challenge: Look through a newspaper or a magazine or listen to a television or radio news report to choose three topics related to the five themes of geography. Then limit the topics to ones you could easily write about in a one-page paper. List the topics on a separate sheet of paper.

Prewriting: Considering Your Audience

Before you start writing, you need to think about who will read what you write. If you're writing a journal entry, your audience will be yourself. If you're writing a research report, your audience will most likely be your teacher. For a report to be read to or shared with the class, your audience will be your classmates. For a letter sent for publication in a newspaper, your audience will be the general public.

Why do you need to consider your audience? The reason is that your audience affects what you say and how you say it. When considering your audience, you need to ask the following questions:

- Will your writing be read by one person or by many?
- What topics will interest your audience?
- How much knowledge does the audience have of your subject?
- How much detail do you need to present?
- Does the language need to be formal or can it be informal?
- What level of vocabulary is appropriate?

Directions: Consider the audience for each of the situations described below. For each one, describe what effect the audience will have on the way you approach your writing, on what you write about, and on the general tone and language.

1. You're writing a personal letter to a friend who has just moved to another state.

   _____

   _____

2. You're writing an essay on a midterm examination. _____

   _____

3. You're writing a report that you will read to the class. _____

   _____

4. You're writing a movie review for the student newspaper.

   _____

   _____

5. You're writing a poem in a birthday card for an eight-year-old female cousin.

   _____

   _____

6. You're writing a letter to a state representative inviting him or her to attend a school function.

   _____

   _____

Reading and Writing Skills

Prewriting: Considering Your Purpose

To write well, you need to identify your purpose in writing. What do you hope to achieve? Considering your purpose will help you choose the appropriate language, style, tone, and approach for your writing. People have many different reasons for writing. Here are some of them:

- To express thoughts
- To share experiences
- To entertain
- To teach or inform
- To express feelings
- To express opinions
- To persuade people to a point of view
- To demonstrate knowledge or understanding
- To urge people to take action

Directions: For each situation described below, identify and describe the person's purpose in writing.

1. Matthew is writing a report on the 1993 flooding of the Mississippi River. He will read his report to the class.

   _____

   _____

2. Karen is writing a letter to her grandmother to tell about her vacation in Florida.

   _____

3. Damon is writing a letter to his local newspaper in which he is asking for volunteers to help with a community fund-raising effort.

   _____

   _____

4. Alicia is writing an editorial in the school newspaper in which she is criticizing students who smoke cigarettes.

   _____

   _____

5. José is writing an e-mail message to all his friends to tell them that he has found a part-time job.

   _____

   _____

6. Kate is writing an advertisement for her lawn-care service. _____

   _____

Prewriting: Gathering Details

Before you begin writing, you need to gather together the details you will include. For a letter, this may simply involve jotting down a few ideas from your head. For an essay or a report, however, gathering details generally involves library research. In the reference section of your library, you will find a variety of materials grouped according to the kinds of information they contain.

Almanacs contain facts and statistics on a wide variety of subjects. They are usually published yearly.

Atlases contain many kinds of maps, with information on climate, population, vegetation, land use, and other topics related to geography's five themes.

Biographical dictionaries present information about prominent individuals, current or historical.

Encyclopedias contain articles with information on a wide range of subjects. Some are updated every year, so look for the most recent volumes.

Geographical dictionaries identify location and may provide brief economic, political, historical, or cultural information about a place.

Information in a dictionary or an encyclopedia is listed by topic in alphabetical order. To locate information in an almanac or an atlas, use the index, generally found at the end of each volume.

Directions: Name one or more reference sources you could use to find information about each of the following topics.

1. history of the Hudson Bay Company _____

2. career of former President George Bush _____

3. population statistics for the 50 states _____

4. locations of Inowroclaw, Poland _____

5. location of mineral resources in North America _____

6. history of fur trading in North America _____

7. U.S. imports and exports, by category, over a 10-year period _____

8. what the Riviera region is _____

9. explorations of Meriwether Lewis _____

10. short history of New Harmony, Indiana _____

11. profile of your state _____

Challenge: Go to your library, and locate the reference section. Find four reference sources that might be helpful in writing a paper on a geographic theme. On a separate sheet of paper, record the title, date, and volume of each publication.

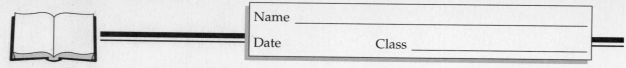
Reading and Writing Skills

Drafting: Organizing Details

A well-written paper is similar to a prize-winning photograph. The main topic or subject is clearly presented through the way details are arranged and displayed. Once you've completed your research and gathered the details, you need to organize them so that your writing will flow smoothly. Here are two techniques that may help you.

Clustering. This is a one-step method for sorting facts or ideas about a topic into related groups, or "bubbles." The writer records the topic in the middle of a page, then thinks of aspects of the topic that should be covered in the paper. Clustering helps the writer see patterns within the topic, and these patterns, in turn, may generate even more ideas. Below is an example of clustering.

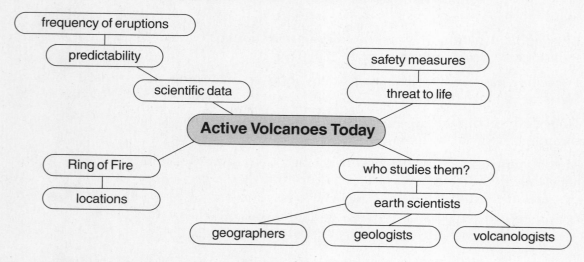

Mapping. This is a two-step way to identify and organize main ideas and supporting details. First, the writer jots down a list of words or phrases related to the topic. Then, the writer makes a "map" to arrange those key words into categories. Below is an example of mapping.

Active Volcanoes Today	
Positive effects	Negative effects
create new land	are deadly
enrich soil	destroy property
attract tourists	contribute to air pollution

Directions: On a separate sheet of paper, discuss in what ways clustering and mapping are similar and in what ways they differ. Which would you prefer to use? Why?

Challenge: Use clustering or mapping to identify and organize ideas about one of the following topics: types of forests, biomes, climate zones, geographic zones, weathering, plate tectonics.

Social Studies Skills Handbook

Drafting: Essay Writing

You've gathered the details, and you've organized them. Now, it's time to write the first draft of your essay. An essay usually has three main parts: an introduction, a body, and a conclusion. This work sheet focuses on the first two parts. You'll learn about writing a conclusion on a different work sheet.

Introduction. The goal of the introduction is to present the subject and gain the reader's interest. Usually, the introduction contains the thesis statement, which is also the topic sentence of the introductory paragraph. You can remember the elements of a good introduction with the letters *ABC:*

- *A*udience appeal—an opening statement that "hooks" the readers and makes them want to read on
- *B*ackground information—one or two statements that support the thesis statement
- *C*larity of purpose—a thesis statement that clearly identifies the main idea of the essay

Body. The body is the main part of the essay. It presents the information that supports the thesis statement in the introduction. The body is composed of a series of related paragraphs. Each paragraph contains a topic sentence or a main idea and other sentences that support the topic or add information about the idea.

Directions: Read the following introductory paragraph to identify the *ABC* elements listed above. Then, answer the questions. Finally, use your textbook to find information for a follow-up paragraph. Write your paragraph on a separate sheet.

Africa is rich in natural resources, yet it is not rich. Many African governments believe modernization is the key to wealth and to improving life for their people. However, this process is difficult and expensive. The governments must learn which aspects of modernization work and which do not through a painful process of trial and error.

1. What gives this paragraph audience appeal? _____

   _____

2. What statements support the main idea of the paragraph? _____

   _____

3. Which sentence provides the thesis statement? What is the main idea of the paragraph?

   _____

   _____

4. What will the body of this essay present? _____

   _____

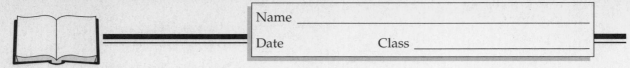

Reading and Writing Skills

Drafting: Writing the Conclusion

A conclusion is an ending. The ending of a story, of a thrilling sporting event, or of summer vacation may leave you happy or sad, bored or intellectually challenged. But whenever an ending works well, it is satisfying.

A strong conclusion for an essay restates the main idea or the thesis statement. It may offer a solution to a problem, challenge the reader to take some type of action, or leave the reader with a thought-provoking message. Here are some guidelines for writing a conclusion.

- Limit the conclusion to one paragraph.

- Restate—but reword—the thesis statement from the introduction.

- Briefly summarize the most important facts or ideas from the body. Don't introduce new or unrelated subjects.

- To leave the reader with a satisfying sense of conclusion, add "punch" to your final sentence. However, don't introduce a tone that doesn't suit the rest of your essay.

Directions: Read and compare the two conclusions below. Circle the one you think is better. On the lines below, explain your selection.

Conclusion A

Unfortunately, such violence between Hindus and Sikhs continues. The recent riots described here serve to highlight the key role religion continues to play in South Asian life and culture. They also serve as a lesson in how easily religious zealots can manipulate the situation. Whether the main goal of these zealots is to gain power or to spread peace will be revealed by the bloodshed they leave in their wake.

Conclusion B

And so it seems that religion and political conflict have always gone hand in hand. As I have pointed out in this essay, this is particularly true of South Asia. It is also my opinion that this type of conflict is the most difficult to resolve.

_____

_____

_____

_____

_____

Challenge: Suppose you have just written an essay about India's caste system. Follow the guidelines above to help you write a conclusion for your essay.

Revising: Editing Your Work

Once you have written the first draft of an essay or a report, you are ready to revise it—to make sure that what you have written is complete and correct. One useful procedure is to review your paper's organization first, then revise for content, and, finally, check—and change, if necessary—grammar, spelling, and punctuation.

Some writers find it helpful to set the piece of writing aside and take a short break before revising it. If you are writing an essay on a test, go on to another question. If the essay is due at a later time, set it aside for a few hours or even a day or so. When you read your piece again with a fresh perspective, you'll be able to analyze it more objectively.

Begin editing by asking the following questions:

- Is the main idea stated in the introduction?
- Do the paragraphs follow a logical order?
- Are the paragraphs smoothly connected with transitional devices?
- Does the conclusion sum up the ideas in the rest of the paper without introducing any new facts or ideas?

Directions: In the following essay about Gandhi's role in winning India's independence from British rule, the main idea is stated in the introductory paragraph. Use the questions listed above to edit the rest of the essay. Reorder paragraphs or sentences, cross out unnecessary details, and add information as necessary.

During the late 1800s, the English-speaking middle class of India developed a strong sense of nationalism and a yearning for greater self-government. This goal might never have been achieved without a young lawyer, Mohandas Gandhi, who led India's struggle for independence from Britain.

In 1935, the British government gave in to mounting pressure and agreed to establish provinces that were governed entirely by Indians.

Gandhi's most powerful weapon against British control was his belief in nonviolent resistance. He urged people not to buy British goods, pay taxes, or serve in the British army. The number of those who adopted his beliefs and actions grew over the years.

This was the first step toward full Indian independence. Not until 1947, a year before Gandhi's death, did India finally win independence. Gandhi's belief that peace and love were more powerful than violence was finally vindicated. In 1982, a movie was made about Gandhi's struggle, starring Ben Kingsley.

© Prentice-Hall, Inc.

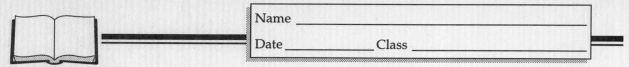
Reading and Writing Skills

Revising: Proofreading

The last step in the revising process is to proofread your final draft. This is an opportunity to identify and correct mistakes. Effective proofreading presents your writing in the best possible way.

Here are some marks professional proofreaders use as they revise written copy before publication. The marks indicate where and what changes are to be made in written manuscripts.

∧ insert	∼ transpose	*cap* capitalize	*lc* make lower case
ℓ delete	⊙ add period	⊂ close up space	*⅌* begin paragraph

Here are some sentences badly in need of editing.

Dispite the diferences in thier ethnic make-up, vietnam laos and cambodia have a great deal in common. The cultures of all three Counrties were infleuncd by India

Now see how a proofreader has marked them for improvement.

⅌ Dispite the diferences in thier ethnic make-up, vietnam, laos, and cambodia have a great deal in common. The cultures of all three Counrties were infleuncd by India⊙

Here is the corrected version.

Despite the differences in their ethnic makeup, Vietnam, Laos, and Cambodia have a great deal in common. The cultures of all three countries were influenced by India.

Directions: Use proofreaders' marks to show where and how to correct the mistakes in the paragraph below. Then, write the corrected paragraph on a separate sheet of paper.

Laos Cambodia and Viet Nam all under Communist control by 1976.

The new govermnents attaked their non-communist residents

hundreds of thousands were killed about 1 million refugees fleed

their homelands. Many ecsaped in small over crowded boats.

thousands drowned. other refugees fled to thailand

Challenge: Use proofreaders' marks to edit a draft of your own writing.

Publishing and Presenting Your Writing

Just as a performance of a play follows many hours of rehearsals and a recital follows many hours of piano practice, publishing—or presenting in final form—follows your hard work of writing a paper. Now the rest of the world (or at least your teacher, family, and friends) will see what you've been up to. Your paper deserves the best presentation you can give it. This does not have to be elaborate, but it should be neat, clean, and attractive.

Publishing may involve several simple steps.

Step 1. Handwrite, type, or input your paper neatly using clean paper. Include margins on both sides, and do not crowd too much on one page. Be sure any divisions between sections of the paper are clear. Review your work for typographical errors.

Step 2. Leave space where necessary, and insert any original illustrations or appropriate graphics, such as maps, diagrams, tables, or charts, that you have traced, copied, or reproduced. Be sure to include information about your sources.

Step 3. If you have done research for your paper, list the books and articles you used in a bibliography at the end. The items should be listed in alphabetical order, according to the last name of the author.

Step 4. Select the location for page numbers (top right corner, bottom right corner, middle of the bottom of the page, etc.), and number your pages consecutively, beginning with the first page of actual writing.

Step 5. Make a cover sheet for your paper. A cover sheet usually includes the title of the paper, your name, the date, the name or the number of your course, and your teacher's name. You may want to vary the size, style, and placement of the lettering or type on your cover sheet. You may also want to use a subtitle and some kind of illustration to dress up your presentation. (Your teacher will instruct you as to the specific information to include on this page.)

Step 6. If appropriate, place your paper in a protective plastic or paper cover or in a folder.

Directions: Draw up a publishing checklist to follow before turning in a final paper. You may want to design your checklist as a series of questions.

Challenge: Practice making attractive cover sheets for papers. Think of three topics you would enjoy writing about, and then design covers for them.

© Prentice-Hall, Inc.

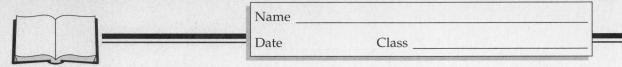

Reading and Writing Skills

Determining Tone, Purpose, and Audience

Tone, purpose, and audience are closely related to one another. The tone of your writing is determined by what your purpose is and who your intended audience is. Similarly, the purpose of your writing will determine the audience you will write for. When preparing to write, you need to consider all three elements.

Directions: The tone, purpose, and audience for two sample writing projects are given below. Study the samples. Then, indicate tone, purpose, and audience for the examples that follow.

Toni is writing an article for her school newspaper in which she is calling for volunteers to help the student government raise money for a new basketball court. Specifically, she needs students to help at a weekend car wash.

Tone: informal, persuasive
Purpose: to provide information and persuade volunteers to give up some of their free time
Audience: fellow students

Paul is hoping to spend a semester at a school in England and has been asked to write an essay as part of his application. In his essay, he must describe what he hopes to gain from his overseas experience.

Tone: formal, respectful, optimistic
Purpose: to show worthwhile expectations; to gain acceptance for his application
Audience: the individual or committee that is considering the application

1. Kelly is writing a story for children that she hopes to get published. It tells of a young city boy who goes to stay with his grandfather on a farm.

   Tone: _____

   Purpose: _____

   Audience: _____

2. Sam has just completed a week of soccer camp and is writing an e-mail letter to his older brother who is away at college.

   Tone: _____

   Purpose: _____

   Audience: _____

3. Lauren has volunteered to write to local business leaders to invite them to be guest speakers in the school's career education classes.

   Tone: _____

   Purpose: _____

   Audience: _____

Writing to Persuade

When you write to persuade, you try to convince people to agree with your opinion. You are surrounded by examples of persuasive writing. Look in a newspaper or a magazine. Read the advertisements, the movie reviews, the letters column, the political speeches. People are constantly trying to persuade you to try something, buy something, or do something. Chances are that you often want to persuade others to your point of view too.

What makes effective persuasive writing? You need to state your point of view clearly, consider your audience, gather evidence to support your argument, and present the evidence in a convincing way. You also need to consider the opposing viewpoint. That way, you can anticipate the arguments against your case and provide counter-arguments.

Directions: Practice writing to persuade by choosing one of the situations below, or use your own idea. Use the spaces provided to state your point of view, list the ideas that support your opinion, and list possible counter-arguments. Then use a separate sheet to write your first draft.

- You're writing to a friend to persuade him or her to visit you during his or her vacation.

- You're writing a speech that you will give to a class of fifth graders in which you will persuade them to wear protective biking gear.

- You're writing an article for the school newspaper in which you want to persuade students to spend less time watching television and more time participating in school sports programs.

- Your own idea: _____

Point of view to be expressed:

_____

_____

Ideas to support point of view:

_____

_____

_____

_____

Possible counter-arguments:

_____

_____

_____

_____

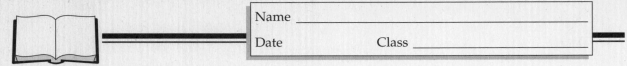

Reading and Writing Skills

Writing to Present Information

When your purpose in writing is to present information—to inform or explain—you need to organize your writing carefully. This kind of writing is based on facts rather than opinions, so it generally requires research and careful planning.

You write to present information when you explain a process or describe the steps involved in making or doing something. You present information when you write a summary of an event or a movie or a book. You present information when you write a definition of something or describe the features of something. Your purpose is to present information in such a way that your audience will understand what you are communicating.

Directions: Practice writing to present information by choosing one of the topics below, or use your own idea. Do research if you need to. Then, use the spaces provided to identify your purpose and your audience and to summarize the facts you will include. When you are satisfied that you have enough information to present, organize your ideas. Then, use a separate sheet to write your first draft.

- Write a summary of a movie that you saw recently, explaining the plot and the characters.

- Write to explain to someone from out of town how to get from your home to your school.

- Describe the steps involved in preparing a sandwich (choose your own sandwich fillings, or choose another dish if you wish).

- Describe the main attractions of your community for someone who has just moved into the neighborhood.

- Your own idea: _____

Topic: _____

Purpose in writing: _____

_____

Audience: _____

Facts to include:

_____

_____

_____

_____

_____

_____

_____

Writing to Describe

Writing to describe involves creating a picture for your readers. You use words to explain how something looks, smells, tastes, sounds, or feels. You can see examples of descriptive writing all around you: advertisements describe the products they are promoting; catalogs describe the goods businesses are trying to sell; newspapers and magazines describe events and people. Description is an important element of any type of writing.

When you write to describe, you use images that your reader can relate to. You select details that will make your description vivid. You organize your description so that one idea builds on another.

Directions: Practice writing to describe by choosing one of the topics below, or use your own idea. Use the spaces to identify your purpose and your audience and to list the ideas and images you will include. When you are satisfied that you have gathered all your ideas and images, organize your material. Then, use a separate sheet of paper to write your first draft.

- For a visiting relative, write a description of a building in your community that interests you.
- Write to a friend, describing the natural features of your community or of a place you visited recently.
- Describe to a friend a vacation that you particularly enjoyed.
- For a school project, describe a person or a place from your past.
- Your own idea: _____

Topic: _____

Purpose in writing: _____

Audience: _____

Ideas and images to include:

_____
_____
_____
_____
_____
_____
_____
_____
_____
_____
_____

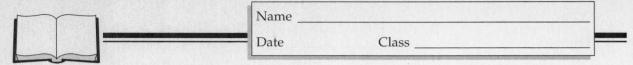
Reading and Writing Skills

Writing Stories

Writing a story involves using your imagination to create a plot or a story line, characters, places, and all kinds of details. Some parts of the story can be based on real places and events, but the basic story must come from your imagination. Stories can range in length from a few pages to more than 1,000 pages. If you are interested in writing stories, you may want to start with shorter stories and work your way up to longer ones.

As with other forms of writing, story writing involves a purpose and an audience. Story writers generally have a target audience in mind. The audience may be young children, teens, or adults. Within those broad categories, the audience may be fans of science fiction, of romance novels, of historical novels, or of stories about animals. The story writer's purpose may be to inform, to amuse, to entertain, to inspire, or a combination of these and other purposes.

Directions: Use your own life experiences as the basis for a short story. Choose one of the topics below, and think about how you could convert it into a short story. Use the spaces to identify your purpose and your audience. Then, describe the basic plot for your story, and list the characters you will include. When you are satisfied with your plan, use a separate sheet to write a first draft of your story.

- What was the most exciting place you ever visited? Use it as the basis for a story.

- Choose a natural disaster—such as a hurricane, a tornado, a volcano, or a flood—that you experienced or that people you know experienced. Write a story about a disaster.

- Do you know someone who moved into your community from another country? Write a story about making friends with a person from a different cultural background.

Purpose of story: _____

Audience: _____

Basic plot: _____

_____

_____

Main characters (names and descriptions):

_____

_____

_____

_____

_____

© Prentice-Hall, Inc.

Writing Plays

Writing a play involves using your imagination to create a plot, a cast of characters, and a script. Play writing also involves describing stage sets and giving stage directions. That way, when the play is performed, the cast members will know exactly what is expected of them.

To write a play, the playwright needs a purpose and an intended audience. The audience may be a particular age group, a particular ethnic group, or a particular community group, such as an elementary school or a senior citizens group. The playwright's purpose may be to amuse, to inform, to entertain, to inspire, to shock, or a combination of these or other purposes.

Plays involve spoken words. Therefore, when writing the script, the playwright needs to be able to mimic the way people speak. He or she also needs to construct the play so that it reveals the personalities of the characters through their actions and words and through the comments of other characters.

Directions: Use a topic you feel strongly about as the basis for a play. Choose one of the topics below, and think about how you might convert it into a short play, or choose another topic. Use the spaces to identify your purpose and your audience. Then, describe the basic plot for your play, and list the characters who will take part. When you are satisfied with your plan, use a separate sheet of paper to write the first draft of your play.

- You have become concerned about the amount of pollution in a nearby body of water. Write a play in which you deal with opposition in trying to protect the water supply.
- Your school has been asked to collect canned food for poor people in the community. Write a play in which students brainstorm ideas for a successful food collection drive.
- A park in your neighborhood has been closed after repeated acts of vandalism. Characters in your play are lobbying to have the park reopened.
- Your own idea: _____

Purpose of play: _____

Audience: _____

Basic plot: _____

_____

_____

Main characters (names and descriptions): _____

_____

_____

_____

_____

Study and Research Skills

Using Your Textbooks

Your textbooks are valuable tools that can help you grasp concepts and gain understanding. To get the most out of textbooks, you need to know how to use them properly. If you take the time to familiarize yourself with the organization and features of a typical textbook, you will save time when you are using the book for studying.

Directions: Choose one of your textbooks for review. Examine it carefully, and answer the questions that follow.

1. What is the title of the textbook you have chosen? _____

2. What kinds of items, other than chapter titles, are listed in the table of contents?

   _____

   _____

3. What information appears on the opening page of each chapter?

   _____

4. What types of special features appear in this textbook?

   _____

   _____

5. What types of questions and activities appear at the end of each chapter?

   _____

   _____

   _____

6. On what page does the Glossary begin (if present)? _____

7. On what page does the Index begin (if present)? _____

8. Does your book have a reference section or appendices? If so, what is included?

   _____

9. What is the advantage of scanning the headings in a chapter before you begin to read it?

   _____

   _____

10. What is the advantage of scanning the illustrations in a chapter before you begin to read it?

   _____

Using the Library

A library is a source of vast amounts of information. To use it efficiently, you need to know how it is organized and how you can use its resources. All of the books, magazines, and reference materials in the library are arranged according to a system that is easy to use. Once you know what you want, you should be able to find it easily—provided that you understand the system.

Directions: Read about the library organization systems below, and visit your school or local library. Then, complete the activities. Use a separate sheet of paper for your answers.

Dewey Decimal System. Every book in the library has a number, and the numbers are arranged in sequence. In most libraries, the numbering system is the Dewey Decimal System. This system groups books into 10 major categories:

000-099	General Works	500-599	Pure Sciences
100-199	Philosophy	600-699	Applied Sciences/Technology
200-299	Religion	700-799	The Arts
300-399	Social Sciences	800-899	Literature
400-499	Language	900-999	Geography/History

Each major category is then divided into subcategories. This system ensures that books on similar subjects are grouped together.

The Library Catalog. The Dewey Decimal System will help you find the area of the library where the book you want is located. The library catalog will give you specific titles, with their numbers. The catalog is a complete list of all the books in the library. Some libraries still have card catalogs, but others have put their catalogs on a computer. When using a computer catalog, you look for a book by instructing the computer to search for a title, an author, or a subject.

Other Resources. Most libraries also have newspapers, periodicals, and pamphlets. Some have computerized indexes to these resources, while others have large printed indexes.

1. Draw a sketch to indicate the general layout of your school or local library. Your layout should show the location of books in the categories listed above, works of fiction, magazines and periodicals, reference books, books on computers, and so on.

2. Briefly describe the library's catalog system for books. Is it a card catalog or a computer catalog? What do you need to know in order to use it?

3. Briefly explain how the newspapers and periodicals in the library are organized and how they are indexed.

Study and Research Skills

Using Catalogs and Indexes

To make the best possible use of your library, you need to be completely familiar with its catalogs and indexes. That way, you can locate a specific book very quickly, find a variety of books on the subject you are researching, or locate suitable articles from newspapers and periodicals.

Directions: Read the following information about catalogs and indexes, and visit your school or local library. Then, answer the questions. Use a separate sheet of paper if you need more room.

Using Catalogs. Some libraries have card catalogs, while others have their catalogs on computer. Both types of catalogs list all the books in the library. With both types of catalogs, you can search for a book by title, author, or subject. The card or the computer screen will give you basic information on a book: title, author, copyright date, subject matter, and a brief description. It will also give the Dewey Decimal System number for the book. If you want to look at the book, write down the number. Then, find the book on the appropriate shelf, or request it from the librarian.

Using Indexes. Newspaper and periodical indexes are located in the reference section of the library. These indexes offer a way of finding current information on a wide range of topics from a variety of sources. Newspaper indexes are listings of important articles published in specific newspapers. Periodical indexes provide listings of articles appearing in a variety of magazines. Increasingly, libraries are using computer-based indexes instead of printed indexes. The most widely used printed index to periodicals is the *Reader's Guide to Periodical Literature.* Various other computer-based indexes are available.

Newspaper and periodical indexes are organized alphabetically by subject. Computer indexes have many advantages over printed indexes in that they offer you a variety of ways of searching for information on the topics that interest you.

Most newspaper and periodical indexes provide citations or abstracts— short descriptions or summaries of the article in question. If you want to see the whole article, you will need to locate the actual newspaper or periodical or locate the article on microfilm. Some new computer indexes include complete articles instead of citations.

1. Describe the catalog system at your local or school library. If it is a computer catalog system, list the items it catalogs in addition to the books in the library.

   _____

2. To what indexes does your library subscribe? _____

3. Which newspapers can you access through these indexes? _____

4. What kinds of periodicals can you access? _____

5. Where do you find the actual articles that you want to read? _____

6. Where can you find the *Reader's Guide to Periodical Literature* in your library?

   _____

© Prentice-Hall, Inc.

Name _____

Date _____ Class _____

Using Computers at the Library

By using the computers at your library, you can save time finding information. You may also be able to print out text and graphics that you can use in researching and writing a report. Some library computers even allow you to download information onto your own disk.

Directions: Read the suggestions for finding out more about your library's computers, and visit your local or school library. Then, answer the questions that follow.

To make the best possible use of the computers at your library, you need to know what capabilities they have. If necessary, ask your librarian to "walk you through" the library's computer systems.

Begin with the computer catalog. Find out how to search for a subject, title, and author. See if the computer also offers a key-word search (which is useful if you remember a word in a title but not the whole title). Find out if the computer offers other services, such as a dictionary, a guide to community services, information on books in other libraries, or an audio and video index.

Next, find out how to use the computer indexes to newspapers and periodicals. Find out how to search for articles, how to view the full text of the articles, how to mark items that you want to print or download, how to print bibliographies, and so on. When you are familiar with the systems offered at your library, answer the questions below.

1. What do you need in order to use your library's computer catalog?

   _____

2. What services, other than the basic catalog, does the computer catalog offer?

   _____

   _____

3. Apart from the computer catalog, what other computer services does the library offer?

   _____

   _____

4. For each of the services listed in item 3 above, briefly describe how to use the service, and give examples of projects for which it would be useful. Use a separate sheet for your answers if you need more space.

   _____

   _____

   _____

   _____

Study and Research Skills

Using CD-ROM Encyclopedias

CD-ROM encyclopedias offer a means of doing research and gathering information quickly and efficiently. CD-ROM encyclopedias enable you to move from article to article, search for related information, view videos, listen to important speeches, study maps, and do many other research activities. When using a CD-ROM encyclopedia, you need to know what it offers and how to use it. Different encyclopedias vary in the amount and type of information they offer and in the ease of accessing that information.

Directions: Locate a CD-ROM encyclopedia at your school or local library, and answer the questions below. Then, prepare a brief report on your findings.

1. Title and publisher of the CD-ROM Encyclopedia: _____

2. How are the articles organized? _____

3. Do the articles highlight key words through which you can access information?

   _____

4. Which of the following features does the encyclopedia offer? (Check those that apply; add others at the bottom of the list.)

   ❏ lists of related articles   ❏ thesaurus

   ❏ photos   ❏ almanac

   ❏ sound   ❏ biographical dictionary

   ❏ video   Other: _____

   ❏ animation   _____

   ❏ atlas   _____

   ❏ time line   _____

   ❏ quiz   _____

   ❏ dictionary   _____

5. How easy did you find the encyclopedia to use? What did you like about it? What did you dislike?

   _____

   _____

   _____

6. On a separate sheet, prepare a brief report on the encyclopedia you used, highlighting its strengths and weaknesses. Compare your findings with those of students who evaluated other CD-ROM encyclopedias.

Study and Research Skills

Using CD-ROM Atlases

CD-ROM atlases offer a means of exploring the world and gathering information quickly and efficiently. CD-ROM atlases enable you to study maps, learn about cities, gather statistics, see photos and videos, and do many other research activities. When using a CD-ROM atlas, you need to know what it offers and how to use it. Different atlases vary in the amount and type of information they offer and in the ease of accessing that information.

Directions: Locate a CD-ROM atlas at your school or local library, and answer the questions below. Then, prepare a brief report on your findings.

1. Title and publisher of the CD-ROM atlas: _____

2. Which of the following does the atlas offer? (Check those that apply; add others at the bottom of the list.)

❑ world maps

❑ country maps

❑ city maps

❑ political maps

❑ physical maps

❑ national flags

❑ national anthems

❑ place name pronunciation guide

❑ photos

❑ videos

❑ street maps/trip planning

❑ historical or cultural points of interest

❑ statistical graphs and charts

❑ time of day in other countries

❑ currency conversion

❑ distance from city to city

❑ locator globes

Other: _____

_____

_____

_____

_____

3. How easy did you find the atlas to use? What did you like about it? What did you dislike?

_____

_____

_____

_____

_____

_____

4. On a separate sheet, prepare a brief report on the atlas you used, highlighting its strengths and weaknesses. Compare your findings with those of students who evaluated other CD-ROM atlases.

Study and Research Skills

Using the Internet

If you're writing a report and you need up-to-date information, the Internet may be your best resource. Information on the Internet is updated constantly. As a result, facts, statistics, and other data found on the Internet are often the most current available anywhere—more current than you will find in a book, or even in a newspaper or a magazine. The Internet is not organized in a set system as a library is, but you'll find the information you need if you know where to look and how to go about your search.

Directions: Read the descriptions of the Internet and its components below. Then, answer the questions that follow.

The Internet ("Net"). The Internet is a series of computer networks linked to one another around the world. These computer networks are connected by telephone lines, cable, and satellite. There is no company called "Internet"; instead, the "Net" is owned, operated, and maintained by all the individuals who use it. Information on the Internet can be accessed by anyone with a computer, a modem, a telephone line, and a route for connecting to the Internet.

The World Wide Web ("Web"). The World Wide Web is a global information database. It offers information in several ways: in text format, as graphic files (such as photographs), and as audio files (such as songs). The Web makes up a large part of the Internet; about 70 percent of all information searches are handled through the Web. You find information on the Web through the use of "links." Links are parts of Web documents that can lead to other, similar documents.

E-mail. E-mail, or electronic mail, is another part of the Internet that you can use to get information. Probably the most frequently used application on the Internet, e-mail messages can be sent from one computer to another. You can use e-mail to send lists of questions to government agencies or to experts in particular fields. With e-mail, it is possible to send the same message to many people at the same time. They can also use e-mail to send their responses back to you.

1. As a source of information, what advantage does the Internet have over conventional print sources? _____

_____

2. What are Web links? _____

_____

3. What equipment do you need in order to use the Internet? _____

_____

4. What advantages does e-mail have over conventional mail? _____

_____

Doing Searches on the Internet

Research on the Internet can provide information that may not be available anywhere else. Some information found on the Internet, however, may not be accurate and reliable. You may need to use several sources to verify your information. Information provided by professional businesses and organizations is generally more reliable than that provided by individuals.

Directions: Read about World Wide Web search methods below. Then, use a computer with Internet access to complete the activities.

URL. URL stands for Uniform Resource Locator, which is the "address" of a site on the Web. You can recognize the address (usually found at the top of your screen as "location") as a string of characters beginning with *http://* and ending with the specific characters that lead to that site. The easiest way to reach a site is to type in a known URL. For example, the URL *http://naic.nasa.gov* will lead you directly to the NASA Space Center Web site.

Search Engines. Very often, you don't know the URL that will lead you to the information that you need. When this happens, you need to use a "search engine." A search engine is a database on the Web that organizes Web sites according to key words in their files or titles. Some already have categories for you to choose from. In others, you simply enter key words relating to your topics and allow the engine to do the searching for you. This will generate a list of file names for you to choose from. Yahoo! at *http://www.yahoo.com* and Lycos at *http://www.lycos.com* are two examples of search engines.

Links. Once you have found a site relating to your topic, through either its URL or a search engine, it may offer further information through the use of a link. Links are words in a Web document that are often underlined or highlighted in some other way. Choosing a particular link may lead you to another Web site offering more information on the same topic.

1. Once you are connected to the Internet, type in the URL for the Yahoo! search engine. How many categories of links does the menu display?

   _____

2. Choose the link for "Regions." When you have connected to this link, choose the link for "Countries." Pick a foreign country, and choose its link. How many links are displayed for that country? Give two examples. Does the country's Web site have categories for its links, such as business or events?

   _____

   _____

3. Choose one of the links within that country's Web site. What is the purpose of the Web site you have chosen? Toward whom does it seem to be directed?

   _____

   _____

Study and Research Skills

Summarizing and Taking Notes

Whether you use print resources or electronic resources for your research, you need a system for summarizing information and taking notes. That way, you will remember what you read or heard, you will be able to organize the information you gather, and you will be able to go back to your original sources if you need to.

Directions: Read the information below about summarizing and taking notes. Then, answer the questions.

Summarizing. To summarize a long report or an article in an encyclopedia, you start by identifying the main ideas. For each paragraph, write down the main idea, using your own words. Then, think about the statements that support the main idea. Always try to use your own words. If you need to use the exact words of your source, place them within quotation marks. If you use the exact words of your source in your final report, you will need to cite the source with a footnote.

Taking Notes. As you do your research, take notes on material that you might want to use in your report. Note cards are a good choice for taking notes, because you can easily arrange and rearrange the material. Here are some suggestions for organizing your note cards:

• Place the citation information for each source in the upper right-hand corner of each card, giving author, title, and date.

• Place a subject heading in the upper left-hand corner.

• Write the facts or ideas you want to record, noting the page number where the information was found.

• Use quotation marks around exact quotations.

• Use one card for each new subject you find under each source.

When doing your research, be on the lookout for maps, graphs, and charts that will help you understand your topic and that you may be able to include in your report. Be sure to include information about the source of the illustrations in your report.

1. Describe how you would summarize a long report. _____

_____

2. List the information that should be included on a note card. _____

_____

3. Why is it important to use quotation marks around direct quotes from sources?

_____

_____

4. What kinds of graphic aids should you look for? _____

_____

_____

Writing an Outline

Creating an outline will help you organize your research in a logical way. The outline is the skeleton of what you will cover in your paper. It will serve as the framework for what you write.

An outline includes a title and the main topics of your paper. You may want to take them from your guiding questions or from the headings on your note cards. Subtopics follow these headings. Use alternating sequences of numbers (Roman and Arabic) and letters (capital and lowercase).

Directions: Utilize the information on these two note cards to complete the partial framework below of an outline for a research paper on the Age of Exploration.

Improved Sailing Ships   **Henry Portal,** *A Maritime History* p. 16

built better to withstand heavy seas and high winds

invention of lateen sail, which allowed ships to sail against the wind

sternpost rudder, making steering easier

could be armed with cannons for defense

Improved Navigation Aids   **Mary Handy,** *Age of Expansion* pp. 19-24

Portolano charts showing directions along sailing routes

improvements in astrolabes, allowing observation and calculation of the position of celestial bodies

magnetic compass for direction finding

Title: _____

I. Factors Leading to the Age of Exploration

   A. _____

      1. _____

      2. _____

      3. _____

      4. _____

   B. _____

      1. _____

      2. _____

      3. _____

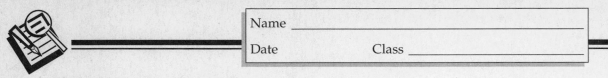

Study and Research Skills

Preparing for Presentations

You've done your research, and you've prepared an outline and a report. Now, you have to present your findings to the class. The keys to making effective presentations are planning and practice. The better prepared you are ahead of time, the more likely your presentation will go smoothly.

Directions: Study the tips below for preparing and presenting a report. Then, complete the activities that follow.

- Organize your main facts and ideas on note cards, using just a few words that will remind you at a glance of what you want to say.

- Prepare a brief, lively introduction that will catch your listeners' attention and give them a framework for listening to your report.

- Prepare a conclusion that rounds off your speech nicely. As with a written report, sum up your ideas in brief, interesting sentences that will help your listeners remember your main points.

- You may want to prepare a graphic to reinforce an important or complicated point. Be sure it can be seen from the back of the room.

- Practice your report at home in front of a mirror. Speak slowly and clearly. Remember that you know your material well, but the audience will hear it for the first time. Vary your tone of voice. Use appropriate hand and facial expressions.

- On the day of your presentation, relax. Refer to your notes to keep your talk flowing smoothly, but do *not* read your cards to the class. Strive to maintain eye contact with your audience. Speak clearly and confidently.

- When you have finished, offer to answer questions.

To prepare for giving your own oral report, remember times when you have been in an audience yourself. Then, complete the activity that follows on a separate sheet of paper.

1. Think of a time when you listened intently to every word a speaker was saying. List some reasons you were interested in the speaker's presentation.

2. Think of a time when a speaker nearly lulled you to sleep. List some reasons you lost interest in the presentation.

Challenge: Practice your speaking skills at home. Select a passage from your textbook, a newspaper, or a magazine. Read it aloud in front of a mirror. Pay special attention to speaking slowly and clearly and to giving meaning to the words with your voice. Also, watch your eye contact, facial expressions, and body language. Try to see and hear yourself as others will.

Concentrating

If you have problems concentrating, you need to identify the kinds of things that distract you. People who are able to concentrate have learned to eliminate or block out distractions. Examples of some of the things that might distract you are listed below, along with suggestions for dealing with them.

Directions: Use the blanks beside each type of distraction to check off those that apply to you, and add any others that are relevant. Study the suggested solutions. Then, use the questions that follow to prepare your own action plan for overcoming distractions. Use a separate sheet of paper for your answers.

Distractions	Possible Solutions
❏ Noise	Turn off the radio and the television. Ask to be left alone while you are studying.
❏ No place to study	Use the library, or find a quiet corner at home.
❏ Telephone interruptions	Ask friends not to call during certain hours.
❏ Missing materials	Check to make sure you have all you need before you start.
❏ Too much on your mind	Make a list, and figure out priorities.
❏ Bad attitude toward studying	Keep your eye on your goals. Talk with someone about the value of education.
❏ Emotional problems	Seek help. Take action to resolve your problems.
❏ Too focused on personal life	Set aside other times to plan your personal life.
❏ Too tired to study	Figure out how to get more sleep.
❏ Lacking energy	Start a regular exercise program to build your reserves of energy.
❏ Other:	_____
❏ Other:	_____

1. Which of the distractions you have checked above do you need to deal with first? What can you do about it?

2. Which distraction do you plan to deal with next? What will you do about it?

3. To whom can you talk to get help with overcoming your distractions?

4. What other actions can you take to help you concentrate more effectively on studying?

Study and Research Skills

Improving Your Memory

Much of your schoolwork involves memorizing information. It is a good idea, therefore, to learn to remember facts and figures in an organized way. Four rules for improving your memory are described below.

Directions: Study the four rules, and answer the questions below each one.

Rule 1: Use what you want to remember as soon as you can.
For example, when you are introduced to someone, you are more likely to remember the person's name if you repeat it as you shake hands with the person.

1. How can you use this rule to help you remember the names and pronunciations of the main cities in a country you are studying?

   _____

Rule 2: Use the "Association Method" to remember.
Try to associate something visual with names and facts that you learn. To remember that the Nile flows north, note that both *Nile* and *north* begin with the same letter.

2. What associations can you devise to help you remember the facts below?

   The capital of Australia is Canberra. _____

   Canberra has a marine west coast climate. _____

   Canberra is located to the south of Sydney. _____

Rule 3: Use the "Link Method" to remember.
Suppose you want to remember that geographers use remote satellite images, censuses, globes, and maps to study the earth. Picture a geographer standing next to a huge globe that has a satellite circling it, and the geographer attempting to take a census of the number of people drawn on the globe. It doesn't matter if the picture in your mind is ridiculous, as long as it helps you remember.

3. What picture can you visualize that will help you remember that Australia is the world's leading exporter of wool?

   _____

Rule 4: Use acronyms and acrostics.
Acronyms and acrostics are simple ways to remember details. You can create a word (acronym) or a sentence (acrostic) made from the first letter of each item you want to remember.

4. Make up an acrostic that will help you remember the five themes of geography: place, location, movement, interaction, and regions.

   _____

   _____

Planning Your Time

The key to using your time most effectively is organization. A well-organized person knows how to be realistic about time needs and is able to set aside an appropriate amount of time to accomplish tasks. To find out how best to plan your time, you first need to analyze how you spend it now. Then you can figure out the changes you need to make.

Directions: Keep a time log for a week in which you record all your activities, hour by hour. At the end of the week, analyze your time log to find out when you were wasting time, when you were spending it wisely, and how you could make changes. Then, read the hints for organizing study time below, and answer the questions that follow.

When organizing your time, keep the following in mind:
- Eliminate wasted time.
- Provide time to study or go over notes each day.
- Set aside at least 30 minutes to work on a task with no interruptions.
- Provide time for short breaks from study.
- Schedule more difficult tasks early in the day or when you are wide awake.
- Be realistic about the total amount of time you should spend studying.

1. According to your log, how much time did you spend studying? _____

2. Do you think you need to expand on this time? _____

   If so, by how much? _____

3. What activities do you think were a waste of time? _____

   _____

4. What actions can you take to avoid wasting time in those ways again? _____

   _____

5. How much time did you spend watching television? _____

6. Do you think that was too much time? Too little? Just right? _____

   In what ways might you change your television viewing habits? _____

   _____

7. What activities do you need to cut back on? _____

8. How can you make those cutbacks? _____

   _____

9. What activities do you need to spend more time on? _____

10. How will you make time for those activities? _____

    _____

11. Summarize the changes you need to make in order to plan your time more effectively.

    _____

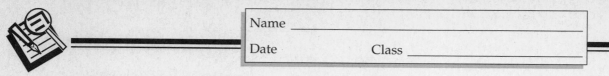

Study and Research Skills

Preparing for a Test

Preparing for a test calls for long-range planning, short-range planning, and planning for the test time itself. By paying attention to each aspect of test preparation, you can greatly improve your chances of doing well on the test.

Directions: Read the guidelines for each phase of test preparation, and answer the questions that follow. Use a separate sheet of paper for your answers.

Long-Range Planning

- Give yourself plenty of time to prepare for the test. Don't leave everything until the night before the test.
- Set aside blocks of uninterrupted time for studying, with short breaks at regular intervals.

  1. Based on your experience in the past, what changes do you need to make to the way you study for a test so that your long-range planning will be better next time?

Short-Range Planning

- If you prepared in advance, do something relaxing on the night before the test.
- Get a good night's sleep before the test.
- Eat a nutritious meal before the test.
- Wear comfortable clothing on the day of the test, and make sure you have all the equipment you need.

  2. Based on your experience of tests in the past, what changes do you need to make to your short-range planning?

  3. On a separate sheet, write a list of the things you need to do during the 24 hours before your next test. Place the sheet in a safe place so that you can refer to it when you need to.

During the Test

- Read the directions carefully.
- Read each question carefully.
- Answer the "easy" questions first. Then, go back to the ones that will take you more time.
- Pace yourself, and be sure to set aside enough time for the essay questions.

  4. Based on your past experience of tests, which kinds of questions caused you the greatest difficulty?

  5. What can you do now to prevent those difficulties in the future?

Map and Globe Skills

Using the Map Key (page 3)

1. manufacturing and trade
2. dotted lines
3. along the coast in the southeast
4. an oil derrick
5. in the northwest and northeast
6. forestry
7. in the northeast
8. tungsten

Using the Compass Rose (page 4)

1. northwest (or north)
2. northwest
3. northeast
4. southern
5. east
6. southeast

Using the Map Scale (page 5)

1. 785 miles (accept answers from 750 to 800); 1,256 kilometers (accept answers from 1,200 to 1,300)
2. 1,238 miles (accept answers from 1,150 to 1,250)
3. Madrid
4. 1,808 miles (accept answers from 1,750 to 1,850)
5. 1,362 kilometers (accept answers from 1,300 to 1,400)

Comparing Maps of Different Scale (page 6)

1. It shows Kuwait's location and size in relation to neighboring countries.
2. It shows the details of the shape of Kuwait as well as offshore islands and the location of major cities.
3. Map A
4. Map B

Understanding Hemispheres (page 7)

1. the Northern Hemisphere and the Western Hemisphere
2. the Equator
3. the Southern Hemisphere and the Eastern Hemisphere
4. the Indian Ocean
5. the Northern Hemisphere

Understanding Grids (page 8)

1. A4
2. giraffes
3. D2 and B4
4. D2, D1, C1, B1, B2, A1
5. B4, A4, A3, A2, A1

Using a Map Grid (page 9)

1. Conde de Superunda Street and Tacna Avenue
2. D4
3. Emancipation Avenue
4. Camana Street
5. Huallaga Street and Ayacucho Street

Understanding Latitude and Longitude (page 10)

1. lines of longitude or meridians
2. lines of latitude or parallels
3. 45°N latitude
4. 90°W longitude

Using Latitude and Longitude (page 11)

Answers to 1 through 5 are actual coordinates. Accept approximations from students.

1. 35°S, 149°E
2. 38°S, 145°E
3. 12°S, 131°E
4. 31°S, 116°E
5. 27°S, 153°E

Comparing Globes and Maps (page 12)

1. A globe provides more accurate information on shape, size, location, distance, and direction than a flat map.
2. A globe cannot show much detail; it is difficult to carry around; you can see only half the world at any one time.
3. They can be shown in a book; they can be taken on trips; they can show small or large areas.
4. To be useful, they have to be distorted.
5. It shows why map distortions are necessary.

Understanding Projection (page 13)

1. a method of showing the curved surface of the earth as a flat map
2. the areas near the poles
3. a flat-plane projection
4. the Robinson projection

Great Circles and Straight Lines (page 14)

1. The flat-plane polar projection. It would show the shortest distance more accurately as well as the route itself.
2. Possible answer: Belarus, Lithuania, Poland, Germany, Netherlands (or Belgium), France, United States
3. Finland, Sweden, Norway, Greenland, Canada, United States
4. that they are not always accurate representations of distance; that you should know what kind of projection you are looking at when using a map to plot routes or calculate distances

Maps With Accurate Shapes: Conformal Maps (page 15)

1. Antarctica appears to be much larger on the map than it is in reality.
2. Greenland and Africa are similar in size on the map. The globe shows that Greenland is many times smaller than Africa.
3. Shape and direction are correct; distance and size are distorted.
4. Possible answer: Lines of latitude and longitude cross at right angles, as they do on a globe, so sailors can plot an accurate course using a compass.

Maps With Accurate Areas: Equal-Area Maps (page 16)

1. Sizes of landmasses in relation to other landmasses are correct; shape, distance, and direction are distorted.
2. Lines of longitude are curved so that they meet at the poles. The 180° line of longitude appears on both outside edges of the map.
3. The shape of North America on the map is distorted to curve inward toward the center of the map.

Maps With Accurate Distances: Equidistant Maps (page 17)

1. distances between places
2. because it is not possible to show the correct lengths of all lines of latitude and longitude
3. small areas such as parts of cities or towns
4. distances from Paris to some of the surrounding cities
5. distances between buildings and monuments within the city of Paris

Maps With Accurate Directions: Azimuthal Maps (page 18)

1. direction
2. shape and size
3. Antarctica
4. You would fly south along the 60°W line of longitude.
5. You would go south along the 90°W line of longitude.

Reading a Political Map (page 19)

1. a national boundary
2. Spain, France, Italy, Greece
3. France, Germany, Austria, Italy
4. Madrid
5. Berlin
6. Spain

Elevation on a Map (page 20)

1. in the western part
2. 0 to 1,000 feet (0 to 305 m)
3. Edmonton
4. Students should suggest mountains or mountain ranges and narrow coastal plains.

Four Types of Landforms (page 21)

1. Mountains are higher and steeper than hills.
2. Both consist of level land. Plateaus are found at higher elevations than plains.
3. a gap in a plateau cut by a river
4. a pattern of dots
5. because plains are more level than hills and easier, therefore, to farm. Also, many plains have access to water.

Relief on a Map (page 22)

1. Possible answer: Mountains run through the center of the region in the shape of backward C. Mountains also run along the coast of the Adriatic Sea.
2. the Carpathian Mountains and the Transylvanian Alps
3. Shaded relief shows at a glance where mountains appear and the general shape of ranges. It does not show mountain elevations.

Maps of the Ocean Floor (page 23)

1. the Mid-Atlantic Ridge
2. Canary Islands, Madeira Islands, Azores
3.-5. Students should correctly identify the islands named.

Reading a Time Zone Map (page 24)

1. 4 P.M.
2. 1 A.M.
3. 12 noon
4. 1 A.M.
5. 7 P.M.

Reading a Natural Vegetation Map (page 25)

1. Answers will vary.
2. temperate grassland
3. mixed forest
4. California
5. coniferous forests
6. Both have coniferous forests.

Reading a Climate Map (page 26)

1. marine west coast
2. humid continental, subarctic, tundra
3. tundra
4. marine west coast and humid continental
5. Norway, Sweden, Finland

Reading an Economic Activity Map (page 27)

1. nomadic herding
2. commercial farming; subsistence farming; hunting, fishing, and gathering; manufacturing and trade

3. hunting, fishing, and gathering
4. Nigeria
5. commercial farming, subsistence farming, nomadic herding
6. Students' answers should show logical reasoning; this part of Africa is arid desert with little vegetation, and it cannot support a variety of activities.

Reading a Historical Map (page 28)

1. Great Britain
2. Angola, Mozambique, Guinea-Bissau
3. Liberia and Ethiopia
4. France
5. All were German colonies.

Understanding Isolines (page 29)

1. lines on a map that connect points of equal value
2. Isolines that are close together would indicate that the land is steep. Isolines that are close together would mean that there is little distance from one elevation to the next.
3. 1,600 m
4. in the western third of the island
5. the eastern half except the northern coast

Reading a Contour Map (page 30)

1. 50 m
2. 875 m (2,870 feet)
3. different elevations
4. It is steeper in the south.
5. the terrain near Mount Gower
6. the northern side
7. Possible answer: I would probably climb Mount Gower from the northwest side.

Reading a Population Density Map (page 31)

1. under 2 per square mile (1 per sq km)
2. the eastern and the southeastern coasts
3. Settlers first arriving in Australia landed on the coasts. The coasts are more accessible for trade and transportation.
4. People need fresh water to live. Australia's largest river system is in the southeast.

Reading a Temperature Map (page 32)

1. the part closest to the Equator, (Central America, most of South America, Africa, South Asia)
2. the part farthest from the Equator; the polar regions
3. 70°F to 80°F
4. 30°F to 70°F

Reading a Population Distribution Map (page 33)

1. 200,000 persons
2. The most heavily populated area is in south central Mexico. Population is heavier along the coasts and along the eastern and western ends of the border with the United States than in the interior.
3. Mexico City and Guadalajara
4. A population distribution map simply shows where the heaviest and lightest concentrations of people are; a population density map shows the number of people per square mile (sq k).

Reading a Natural Resources Map (page 34)

1. the letter C
2. the Midwest, especially Iowa, Missouri, and Nebraska
3. iron
4. The largest concentration is in Texas and Louisiana.
   Petroleum is also found in the Midwest in Wyoming and the Dakotas as well as along the coast of California.
5. the Rocky Mountains

Understanding Road Maps (page 35)

1. 1, 31, 32
2. route 32
3. Muswellbrook
4. 288 km

Reading a Road Map (page 36)

1. principal highways
2. Any two: Hobart, Fern Tree, Longley
3. Take route B64 from Hobart through Fern Tree and Longley. Turn right onto A6, following it to Huonville (35 km from Hobart to Huonville). Take B68 from Huonville to Cygnet (16 km). Continue on B68 from Cygnet to Snug (49 km). To return, take B68 to Kingston (29 km) and then A6 to Hobart (about 10 km).

Reading an Ocean Currents Map (page 37)

1. the North Atlantic Current
2. the Labrador Current
3. from west to east, and northward
4. The East Australian Current is warm and the West Australian Current is cool.
5. the Gulf Stream
6. the Peru Current

Reading a Wind Map (page 38)

1. the Polar Easterly Winds
2. the Doldrums at the Equator; the Horse Latitudes at the tropics of Cancer and Capricorn (30°N and 30°S)
3. between 30°N and 60°N and 30°S and 60°S
4. from west to east
5. from the east

Reading a Trade Map (page 39)

1. Sardinia and Sicily
2. Carthage
3. the Black Sea
4. Alexandria
5. the Strait of Gibraltar
6. Answers will vary. Students should suggest that by trading over a large area, the Greeks and the Romans developed significant power and influence over other nations.

Critical Thinking Skills

Expressing Problems Clearly (page 40)

1. the decay in forests of the Swiss Alps
2. air pollution, lack of proper care, past forestry practices
3. They have passed strict pollution-control laws, are giving the forests emergency care, and have started reforestation programs.
4. Possible answers: dangers of avalanches, falling rocks, earth slides, flooding

Identifying the Main Idea (page 41)

1. First paragraph: Heavy downpours and flooding caused devastating log slides. Second paragraph: Public outcry about deforestation, along with photographic evidence, led the government to ban commercial logging.
Third paragraph: Logging companies moved to other countries, but the ban was expected to lead to increased illegal logging in Thailand. Fourth paragraph: Deforestation will continue because the ban does not prevent rural villagers from clearing forest land.
2. To prevent further deforestation and in response to a public outcry, Thailand has banned commercial logging operations. This action will help alleviate Thailand's environmental problems but probably will not solve them.

Identifying Central Issues (page 42)

Students should note in their reports that the main purpose of the experimental project was to get rid of malaria-carrying mosquitoes and that the experiment was successful.

Distinguishing Fact from Opinion (page 43)

1. 1, 2, 4, 5
2. Possible answers: encyclopedia, history book, biography
3. 3, 6, 7, 8

4. 7, 8
5. The opinion in statement 7 that Hitler was stubborn is supported by the fact that he refused to leave his headquarters in Berlin when the Soviets arrived. The opinion in statement 8 that Hitler was the most brutal dictator the world has ever known is supported by the fact that he was responsible for the extermination of over six million Jews.

Checking Consistency of Ideas (page 44)

1. to reduce U.S. dependence on foreign energy sources
2. Prudhoe Bay, in the northeast corner of Alaska
3. It is the site of the Arctic National Wildlife Refuge, a wilderness area.
4. Oil development in Alaska is likely to upset the ecological balance in the wilderness area.
5. Answers will vary. Encourage students to look for compromise resolutions such as limited oil exploration or exploration in less environmentally sensitive areas.

Distinguishing False from Accurate Images (page 45)

1. The image of the Caribbean most people have is probably that portrayed in television and magazine advertisements: an idyllic place of white, sandy beaches and crystal-clear, sparkling waters. This passage presents an image of the Caribbean as a region damaged by oil, chemical, and sewage pollution; threatened by resulting health problems; and existing in precarious ecological balance.
2. Possible answer: The source is reliable and well informed on environmental problems. It is a nonprofit research group that advises countries worldwide.
3. The passage describes high levels of spilled petroleum, urban sewage, harmful sedimentation, and toxic agricultural runoff and mining wastes in Caribbean waters.

Identifying Assumptions (page 46)

1. Czechoslovakia's prospects for a peaceful transition from communism to democracy and a free market economy
2. Possible answer: cautiously hopeful
3. The author assumes and states that the transition will not be easy, but does not directly state this assumption.
4. Yes. The author states that "the country's level of economic development, its Western orientation, its developed social structure and its previous experience with democratic political institutions all bode well for the future of democracy."

Recognizing Bias (page 47)

1. Because they believed in white superiority, they ignored the role Africans and Arabs played in the settlement and the exploration of Africa.
2. He views them as self-centered adventurers who went to Africa for riches and fame.
3. Possible answer: They are biased, describing people and interpreting events according to their own values. Often, their view of history is slanted, reflecting a bias toward their own culture over others.

Recognizing Ideologies (page 48)

1. Europeans regarded wives as homemakers and men as breadwinners.
2. Labor was divided more evenly in African societies, with women working the land and living a separate economic life from that of their husbands.
3. The European colonial administrators stressed cash (export) crops and focused their training and financial help on male farmers, since they assumed males would be doing the farming. This left the women farmers poorer and less able to make the investments needed to improve crop yields.

Recognizing Cause and Effect (page 49)

Possible answers:
1. **Effect:** A series of deserts forms around the globe.
2. **Effect:** As the rising air cools, it sheds its moisture as rain.
3. **Cause:** Air loses its moisture as it rises to cross a mountain.
4. **Effect:** People cut down trees in the dry grasslands around the desert.
5. **Effect:** The wind carries away the loose soil, and the land becomes part of the desert.

Predicting Consequences (page 50)

Possible answers:
1. The moderates and the extremists might have struggled over what course India would take to gain independence from the British. Indian Muslims might have agitated for formal laws to ensure their political rights.
2. Indian violence against the British might have increased in angry reaction to the massacre. Indian violence might have decreased because of fear of British repression.
3. Negative world reaction to the behavior of the British might have pressured them to adopt milder penalties against Indian political protesters. The British might have shown an increased willingness to use force, believing it to be the only way to stay in power.

Identifying Alternatives (page 51)

Students' answers will vary. Encourage them to explore the pros and cons of the ideas they submit.

Drawing Conclusions (page 52)

1. Active volcanoes and earthquake zones are frequently located in the same areas.
2. The earthquake zones generally coincide with plate boundaries.
3. The Indo-Australian Plate continues to push against the Eurasian Plate in the region of the Himalayas.

Graph and Chart Skills

Reading a Bar Graph (page 53)

1. Italy
2. Greece
3. Portugal imported 17 billion dollars worth of goods and exported 28 billion dollars worth of goods.
4. Spain
5. Students' graphs should be clear and accurate. Possible conclusion: Summer falls in different times of the year in the Northern and Southern hemispheres.

Reading a Line Graph (page 54)

1. in the 1900s
2. 11 billion people
3. about 2.5 billion people
4. around 1800
5. Answers will vary. Students might suggest that education in developed countries has helped to stabilize population growth, while improved health care in developing countries means that more infants survive and that people live longer.
6. Students' graphs should be clear and accurate. Students should comment on the widening gap between imports and exports.

Reading a Circle Graph (page 55)

1. 17.7 percent
2. 0.3 percent
3. Christians
4. Muslims
5. almost twice as large
6. Students' graphs should be clear and accurate. Students should comment on the fact that Asians outnumber the populations of all other regions combined.

Reading a Diagram (page 56)

1. A strait is a narrow waterway connecting two larger bodies of water; an inlet is a recess in the shoreline.
2. peninsula
3. a group of islands
4. Mountains are higher than hills.
5. An isthmus is a narrow strip of land with water on either side that joins two larger bodies of land.
6. Possible answer: A diagram can give a visual image of what the text describes.

Reading a Flowchart (page 57)

1. It shows the different processes involved in making green tea and black tea.
2. It is simpler and provides a visual image.
3. It could be illustrated with pictures of the tea plant and with equipment involved in the various processes.
4. Students' flowcharts should be clear and accurate.

Analyzing a Photograph (page 58)

1. terraced rice paddies in Indonesia
2. Terracing is a system of making land suitable for agriculture by cutting flat terraces into the sides of hills.
3. The land was too hilly. Without terracing, the soil would wash away. The land could not be flooded for planting rice.
4. Possible answer: The photo indicates that good agricultural land is in such short supply that creating terraces is worth the time and effort it takes.

Analyzing Art (page 59)

1. that it was lonely and primitive and required hard work, but also that it was peaceful and built around the family unit
2. logs and timber
3. from the land surrounding their home
4. an axe for chopping wood and a rifle for hunting
5. They ate the meat of the animals they hunted and eggs from the chickens. They probably grew vegetables and grain, too, though the picture does not show this. The chopped logs and the smoke from the chimney indicate that they burned wood to stay warm.

Analyzing a Political Cartoon (page 60)

1. the United States
2. the star and the stripes on his clothes; the "Uncle Sam" label on the life preserver
3. people desperate to immigrate to the United States because of political, economic, or social conditions in their homelands
4. because he cannot rescue so many people
5. The cartoonist is saying the United States cannot possibly take in all the people who want to immigrate because of conditions in their home countries.

Reading a Time Line (page 61)

1. in 1517
2. 17 years
3. 120 years
4. the Irish rebellion that began in 1916
5. Possible answer: Space exploration has continued steadily since 1961, with just a few periods in which there was little activity.

Reading a Table (page 62)

1. rates of literacy and infant mortality, number of workers in agriculture, and life expectancy for males and females in Costa Rica, Panama, Honduras, and Guatemala
2. Honduras: 43 per 1,000 births; Guatemala: 52 per 1,000 births
3. In all countries, women have a higher life expectancy than men.
4. Generally, a high literacy rate and a low infant mortality rate occur together.
5. Possible answer: The countries with the highest literacy rates have the fewest agricultural workers.
6. Costa Rica. It has the highest literacy rate and life expectancies and the lowest infant mortality rate.

Mean, Median, and Mode (page 63)

1. 2
2. 3
3. 2.5
4. either the mode or the median, because they are better indicators of the fact that the largest number of islands has only 2 hotels
5. the mean, because it is a better indicator of hotel availability throughout the archipelago

Analyzing Statistics (page 64)

Answers will vary, depending on the countries chosen. Encourage students to make comparisons and draw conclusions.

Reading a Climate Graph (page 65)

1. average monthly rainfall and temperatures in Mumbai
2. July
3. January, February, March, April, May, October, November, December
4. June, July, August
5. Temperatures are fairly steady throughout the year, ranging from a low of about 75°F to a high of about 85°F.
6. Possible answer: No. Temperatures fluctuate only 10° all year; rainfall ranges from 0 to 24 inches.

Comparing Climate Graphs (page 66)

1. New Delhi
2. June
3. January and December
4. July
5. about 8 inches
6. Paris
7. Seattle
8. New Delhi
9. Possible answer: Paris has a temperate climate, with moderate seasonal variations and relatively little monthly fluctuation in precipitation.

Reading a Cartogram (page 67)

1. Despite its small size, Japan has by far the largest GNP of any of the countries in the region.
2. Indonesia
3. New Zealand's GNP is, relative to its size, larger than Australia's.
4. Although it is a small country, South Korea's GNP is relatively large.
5. China's GNP is much smaller than that of Japan, even though China is a much larger country.

Reading and Writing Skills

Previewing the Headings and the Pictures (page 68)

Answers will vary, depending on the chapter chosen.

Giving Yourself a Purpose for Reading (page 69)

Answers will vary, depending on the chapter chosen.

Asking Questions While You Read (page 70)

Answers will vary, depending on the chapter chosen.

Connecting Content to What You Already Know (page 71)

Answers will vary, depending on student knowledge and on the chapter chosen.

Predicting What You Will Find Out (page 72)

Answers will vary, depending on the chapter chosen.

Visualizing What Things Look Like (page 73)

Answers will vary, depending on the chapter chosen.

Determining If You Understood What You Read (page 74)

Answers will vary, depending on the chapter chosen.

Demonstrating What You Know (page 75)

Answers will vary, depending on the chapter chosen.

Learning More About a Topic (page 76)

Answers will vary, depending on the chapter chosen.

Overview: The Writing Process (page 77)

1. prewriting, drafting, revising, presenting
2. choose a topic, define its scope, gather information, create an outline
3. during the drafting (writing) stage
4. content, clarity, style, accuracy
5. Answers will vary. Students should suggest that breaking the task of writing a paper into logical, manageable steps makes the work easier. Following the writing process should also improve the quality of the research report.

Prewriting: Choosing a Topic (page 78)

1. b
2. a
3. c
4. b

Prewriting: Considering Your Audience (page 79)

Possible answers:
1. The audience is one person, a friend. You can write about things that will interest the friend, using informal language.
2. The audience is your teacher. Your writing should focus on showing your knowledge and understanding of the subject. The language should be formal.
3. The audience is your classmates. The writing should be formal but engaging and should take into account their current knowledge about the subject.
4. The audience is other students. The writing style should be influenced by the fact that your words are being published, but it can be fairly informal. Your aim is to inform but perhaps also to entertain.
5. The audience is a young girl. The writing should take her age into account; the vocabulary should be simple.
6. The audience is the state legislator and his or her staff. The writing should be formal, polite, informative, and persuasive.

Prewriting: Considering Your Purpose (page 80)

1. Matthew's purpose is to demonstrate knowledge of his subject and to write a report that will interest his classmates.
2. Karen's purpose is to inform, to share experiences, and perhaps to entertain.
3. Damon's purpose is to persuade people to participate in what he considers a worthwhile effort.
4. Alicia's purpose is to express her opinion and to try to persuade people to her point of view.
5. José's purpose is to inform.
6. Kate's purpose is to inform and to attract prospective customers.

Prewriting: Gathering Details (page 81)

Possible answers:
1. encyclopedia
2. biographical dictionary, encyclopedia
3. almanac
4. geographical dictionary, atlas
5. atlas
6. encyclopedia
7. almanac
8. geographical dictionary
9. biographical dictionary, encyclopedia
10. geographical dictionary, encyclopedia
11. encyclopedia, almanac

Drafting: Organizing Details (page 82)

Be sure each student makes a choice of using clustering or mapping for a logical reason: for example, choosing clustering because he or she prefers to visualize patterns, or choosing mapping because he or she prefers two steps to one.

Drafting: Essay Writing (page 83)

1. The opening sentence is simple but powerful and will make readers want to read more.
2. The second and third sentences provide background information leading up to the thesis statement.
3. The last sentence is the thesis statement. The main idea is that the governments are trying different ways of modernizing.
4. Follow-up paragraphs will give examples of successful and unsuccessful efforts to modernize.

Drafting: Writing the Conclusion (page 84)

Conclusion A is better.
Possible explanation: This paragraph is clearly a summary. The reader is left with a useful perspective for understanding developments in South Asia. Conclusion B says very little and has a casual tone inappropriate for a formal essay. There is no satisfying sense of conclusion.

Revising: Editing Your Work (page 85)

Check that students' editing addresses the questions listed in the worksheet.

Revising: Proofreading (page 86)

Possible paragraph:
Laos, Cambodia, and Vietnam were all under Communist control by 1976. The new governments attacked their non-Communist residents. Hundreds of thousands were killed. About 1 million refugees fled their homelands. Many escaped in small, overcrowded boats. Thousands drowned. Other refugees fled to Thailand.

Publishing and Presenting Your Writing (page 87)

Check that students' checklists cover the main points outlined in steps 1-6.

Determining Tone, Purpose, and Audience (page 88)

1. Tone: informal, friendly
   Purpose: to entertain, inform, amuse
   Audience: young children
2. Tone: informal, chatty
   Purpose: to inform, share experiences, stay in touch
   Audience: his brother
3. Tone: formal, respectful
   Purpose: to persuade people to be guest speakers
   Audience: local business leaders

Writing to Persuade (page 89)

Answers will vary.

Writing to Present Information (page 90)

Answers will vary.

Writing to Describe (page 91)

Answers will vary.

Writing Stories (page 92)

Answers will vary.

Writing Plays (page 93)

Answers will vary.

Study and Research Skills

Using Your Textbooks (page 94)

Answers to questions 1 through 8 will vary, depending on the textbook chosen.

9. Students should suggest that scanning the headings will give them a feel for the content and coverage of the chapter.
10. Students should suggest that scanning the illustrations will give them a visual insight into the topic of the chapter.

Using the Library (page 95)

Answers will vary.

Using Catalogs and Indexes (page 96)

Answers will vary.

Using Computers at the Library (page 97)

Answers will vary, depending on the computer services offered by the library.

Using CD-ROM Encyclopedias (page 98)

Answers will vary, depending on the CD-ROM encyclopedia examined.

Using CD-ROM Atlases (page 99)

Answers will vary, depending on the CD-ROM atlas examined.

Using the Internet (page 100)

1. It is updated constantly.
2. parts of Web documents that can lead to other similar documents
3. a computer, a modem, a telephone line, and a route for connecting to the Internet
4. It is quicker, and the same message can be sent to many people at the same time.

Doing Searches on the Internet (page 101)

Answers will vary.

Summarizing and Taking Notes (page 102)

1. Write down the main idea and the supporting statements.
2. author, title, and date; subject; facts or ideas; page number
3. so that sources that are directly quoted in a report can be acknowledged
4. maps, graphs, charts

Writing an Outline (page 103)

Title: The Age of Exploration

I. Factors Leading to the Age of Exploration
   A. Improved Sailing Ships
      1. Ships were built better to withstand heavy seas and high winds.
      2. The invention of the lateen sail allowed ships to sail against the wind, not just downwind.
      3. The sternpost rudder made sailing easier.
      4. Cannons allowed ships to be armed for defense.
   B. Improved Navigation Aids
      1. Portolano charts were developed to show directions along sailing routes.
      2. Improvements in astrolabes allowed observation and calculation of the position of celestial bodies.
      3. Magnetic compasses could be used for direction finding.

Preparing for Presentations (page 104)

Answers will vary.

Concentrating (page 105)

Answers will vary.

Improving Your Memory (page 106)

1. Students might suggest a classroom quiz in which they get to say aloud the names of the cities in response to simple questions.
2. Possible answers:
   Canberra and *capital* both begin with a *C*.
   Canberra is *close* to the *coast* (three *C*s).
   South and *Sydney* both begin with an *S*.
3. Possible answers:
   the shape of Australia in the form of a woolly sheep
   the shape of Australia wrapped in a woolly sweater

4. Possible answer: Purple lilacs may ignore roses.

Planning Your Time (page 107)

Answers will vary.

Preparing for a Test (page 108)

Answers will vary.